DECISIVE

How to Make Breakthrough Decisions

Andrew Horton

Published by Ascerian Inc.
London, Ontario, Canada

Design by Amnet.

Library and Archives Canada Cataloguing in Publication information is
available upon request.

Paperback ISBN: 978-1-7772604-0-8
eBook ISBN: 978-1-7772604-1-5

*For my parents, Roy Horton and Wendy Horton,
who gave me all of my foundations for success.
And for my wife and son, Lisa Horton and Cooper Horton,
who keep me motivated on the journey each and every day.*

CONTENTS

ABOUT THE AUTHOR

Andrew Horton helps leaders change their organizations and the world through better decisions.

As the founder of an exciting new stream of Behavioral Economics—Causal Economics—and an award-winning technology marketing executive with more than twenty years of direct experience in making big impact decisions—Andrew's perspective is unique. His work is published in leading peer-reviewed academic journals and he is regularly called upon to make submissions and review those of other scholars.

Andrew's expertise is constantly in demand from top brands and includes work for a vast array of top brands such as Ceridian, Morneau Shepell, Fairfax Financial, Teknicor/Dell EMC, TD Waterhouse, and CIBC—to name a few.

He holds an advanced economics degree from Western University and an MBA from the Ivey School of Business.

PREFACE

Take a moment. Think of an incredibly successful person? Who comes to mind? Steve Jobs, Oprah Winfrey, Stephen Hawking, Michael Jordan? There are certainly many others. These successful people come from diverse fields. They are/were all smart and worked hard. Yet, there's a deeper common thread—a common thread that guided them and drove them forward.

The common thread is *decisions*. Their decisions brought out their heartfelt passions and turned them into massive, sustained action. They faced very different situations and created very different outcomes, but they each inspire us to make powerful decisions that move us forward to be the best we can be.

Many people see decisions as mundane tasks that we all have to do. I believe differently. To me, decisions are the most important engine of change, in business and social causes. Step back and think about it for a moment—nothing changes without a decision—not a thing. I don't think it's too bold to say that decisions define humanity and our very reality. Do you? Our reality is what we believe and perceive, and the world is shaped only by those who take action.

What do you attribute the success of Steve Jobs to? Luck? Genius? No doubt he had tremendous capabilities, but those would have meant nothing without his decision-making. His decision-making is what put his thoughts into action.

Do you think Winston Churchill, John F. Kennedy, Ronald Reagan, Martin Luther King Jr., or Jack Welch were extremely effective, average, or poor decision makers? Is there anyone in business who is successful in the long term who isn't great at decisions? Decisions about markets to be in, about products to launch, about investments to make? Running a business is always about decisions.

So, do you want to make better decisions? Do you NEED to make better decisions? Are you relying on outdated management and decision theory? What do you dream about? Does it require decisions to get there? Of course, it does.

If you don't yet have a driving ambition—a dream pulling you forward—it's actually decision-making that will guide you to uncovering your calling.

To various degrees, decision-making is contained in the works of masters in personal development and business strategy, like Anthony Robbins, Simon Sinek, Malcolm Gladwell, and others. But I passionately believe that we need a dedicated focus on decision-making.

Thinking and analyzing without action isn't a decision. Acting without thinking and analyzing isn't a decision either. Decision-making is a combination of thinking/analyzing *and* action. If you are a 100 percent shoot-from-the-hip action taker, this book will help you. If you suffer from analysis paralysis, this book will help you too.

DECISIVE lays out the prominent models of decision-making. It's your one-stop shop for insight on the topic. When you're done reading, you can be confident that you'll be up to speed on the latest insights and concepts about decision-making. Hopefully, this in itself is helpful to you, but my goal is to provide you with something more—something groundbreaking—and a personal passion of mine. This book also introduces new insights from the theory of Causal Economics. Causal Economics is a new frontier of the very hot area of Behavioral Economics, launched in an academic peer-reviewed journal. I have the pleasure of authoring that paper, which brings together insights from behavioral economics, two decades of experience as a marketing executive, and a unique academic angle.

I hope you see *DECISIVE* as a chance to master the best of mainstream approaches to decision-making and to gain an edge on your competitors through the innovative new approach of Causal Economics.

INTRODUCTION

DECIDE

Just seeing the word has power. Saying it out loud, you can feel its weight. Inspiring for some, daunting for others. What does it mean to you? Why does this one word hold so much power?

Nothing changes without a decision. It's the core of human experience and meaningful change. Any positive impact in the world results from bold, actioned decisions. Without decisions, the world either stands still or plods along without direction. Worse yet, poor decisions can result in personal and societal catastrophes.

Life Is Decisions. Business Is Decisions. Social Change Is Decisions. Management Is Decisions

I wrote this book because I believe that effective decision-making should be a priority focus for any person who has aspirations. Maybe even the number one focus. It will even help those who haven't yet found their calling or are seeking their vision. There are many amazing self-improvement and management ideas out there. I feel they all require great decision-making to be effective. Here, I'll present an easy-to-use approach that capitalizes on the breakthrough work of masters—Anthony Robbins on "change", Simon Sinek on "why," and others.

Can you benefit from becoming a better decision maker? It's tough to think of another capability one can develop and master that will a have bigger bang-for-the buck, literally. We all make decisions. Our destiny reflects our decisions—or lack thereof. But very few of us make decisions deliberately in line with the most powerful methods. Whether your passion is business, philanthropy, science, or something else, decisions are the only thing that will get you where you want to go.

Do you think you've read enough on decision-making? Well, you haven't really, until you're up to speed on the insights of Causal Economics (CE). CE is a recent branch of decision-making theory based in Behavioral Economics (BE). I had the honor of first introducing the theory through a peer-reviewed academic journal article in April 2019. Books about Behavioral Economics like *Nudge* and *Predictably Irrational* represent a big recent step forward in our understanding of decision-making. However, they don't go far enough in providing a complete and realistic model for decision-making in practice. CE is a bold new way of thinking about decisions with big implications. In this book, you'll learn the simple formula for effective decision-making with sustainable results.

The insights shared here have helped CEOs, athletes, employees, artists, social activists, and even drifters harness the power of effective decision-making to improve their outcomes. If you're a business leader, your profits are directly tied to your organization's decision competency. If you're a social activist, achieving your cause relies on driving necessary behaviors through better decisions. If you're trying to improve your own life, you know in your gut that making the right decisions *is* fundamental.

Reality check—decisions can be tough. That's why we'll look at how to make it much easier to make the right decisions using the insights of CE. We'll also review some of the leading decision-making theories from economics and psychology and illustrate why they haven't provided all the tools you need. That's why you need to understand CE to make better decisions in life.

The aim of *DECISIVE* is to help you get what you really need with a quick read of the core concepts. It also provides a real deep dive for those leaders who want to understand decisions—the fuel of business—far better than their competitors. If you take up decision-making as a core expertise, you'll want to become an expert in all nuances of CE, so you and your organization can stand out and earn a reputation for uncanny insights and predictions about what people in your business are about to do and why.

What Are the Benefits of Better Decision-Making?

Decisions are at the heart of almost every challenge you face. That's because, you require decisions to move to solutions. Is your problem one of the following?

- Revenue growth
- Margin
- Profit
- Competitive threats
- Customer satisfaction
- Product launches
- Social causes
- Many more…

If yes, it's likely really a decision problem.

What's the Cost of Not Being a Strong Decision Maker?

The obvious costs of being a poor decision maker are lost opportunities and higher personal costs. These can be significant, but they are generally restricted to the decision at hand. An often forgotten cost of poor decision-making that can do long-term damage is our reputation. Our true credibility is a reflection of our decisions.

People can judge you on what you say and have an opinion about you, but their willingness to rely on you when they need help will reflect their judgment of how well you make decisions and the nature of those decisions—your vision, your measurable targets, and your demonstrated actions.

Ignore Most of What You Hear
My goal in this book is to help you make better decisions—in order to have the best results. It's not to be political. But I have to call out the reality: today's culture has become very adverse to personal empowerment. It's perhaps hard for people of my age to comprehend, but today people get trophies for "failing." No one can be honest because they will be cancelled or doxed on social media unless they fall in line on the "talk track." Many people believe the world and others are entirely responsible for their shortcomings. They believe that they deserve to be protected from all kinds of pain at all times. This culture is disastrous for our ability to be the best we can be.

Reality is this. You own your destiny. That's not to say that some of us don't start from horrible circumstances with harder battles to overcome. We all have different starting points. Change that brings greater benefits is hard—exercise, building wealth, raising a family, doing philanthropy, and so on. Change that is easy is usually not good for you, like relying on material things for pleasure.

If you take ownership of your future you can live the life *you* want to live. If you want immediate affirmation of how special you are just for being you, put down this book right now—you will be greatly disappointed unless you're willing to change.

The reason you have to ignore most of what you hear in the media and popular culture discussions is because it isn't reality. It is sensationalism. News is a product, made exciting by blowing up the most provocative emotions and story lines. That's why you'll see stories about crime far more often than heroic everyday citizens.

The other thing you have to politely ignore most of the time is the advice of 90 percent of the population you talk to. Most people are not focused in life, and don't have their sights set on a bigger mission. Their actions will reflect that aimlessness. Don't get caught up in it. Role model successful people and stay in that headspace, except when you're doing reverse role modelling, which we'll discuss later.

Simply put, gain requires upfront pain. Resources, effort, and time are not free. That's why impactful decisions are hard. They always have been and always will be.

A Famous Success Decision to Learn From

Who are the most revered business people in our lifetime? Warren Buffet, Steve Jobs, Bill Gates? There are some amazing people to choose from. You may have role modelled them in various ways. Whether your choice is one of these or someone else, I want to briefly look at their success through the lens of decision-making. Too often, we try to learn from others by focusing on the strategies and tactics *they* employ. This is like focusing on symptoms instead of the underlying conditions. The underlying condition in any human endeavor is the decision-making of the person. What they have done is not 100 percent replicable, because their context and timing were unique. There is truth to the expression "the right place at the right time." They certainly adapted to their time, but your time is different from what they faced. Which means your journey to your version of greatness will be different. When role modelling, focus on their mindset and decision-making over the details of the marketplace they faced.

That being said, let's take a deeper look at Steve Jobs from a decision-making perspective. His decisions, like all decisions, started with an underlying vision that he had set his sights on.

Many of us may have our driving visions in place, but many others are searching for theirs. How can we have an impact and feel like our contribution to society matters? If you're doing neither of these, you're drifting and letting others make decisions for you. You'll enjoy life more if you begin your own search for your true driving passion.

Steve Jobs was a man of incredible vision. He wanted to change the world, and felt that a tech company was the way to do it. Jobs is a great example, because he is not someone who was steered into success by circumstances. He wanted it, mapped it out, and grabbed it! This is where nuance matters. Everyone talks about his desire to simplify and beautify customer experience. That is part of it, but they leave out his intense desire to change the world and make a ton of money. If he didn't "do Apple," he would have launched something else. As we know, successful entrepreneurs usually have several previous failures. Their vision, like that of Jobs, is driven by their deepest definitions of success—making money, helping society, and so forth—and they see it happening through exciting ventures they come up with.

You can only ever achieve the level of success you hunger for. This "hunger" is different for everyone.

Jobs' vision was backed by specific targets. Without these, precious (finite) time and energy would be wasted. Targets set the focus needed for achievement. Anyone who says that he or she needs to stay nimble in a rapidly changing world and hence avoid setting targets is delusional. If targets need to change, change them—but you need to have them!

Jobs had a few overriding targets; he took incredible action. His vision, clear targets, and action are the ingredients of truly inspirational and great leadership. It is often said that Apple is a cult, both for employees and customers. You know a brand is phenomenal when people are that loyal. This culture means that Jobs' individual decision was taken up by others. They wanted Apple to succeed and dominate, not just solve their immediate concerns. That's what amplified the decision of one into millions, of corroborating decisions by individuals. Scale. Brand. Profit.

Apple faced its challenges. So did Steve Jobs in his career there. Most of us know he was booted from the company he founded and brought back later to save it. What a perfect example of "reaction." In the face of such a challenge, Jobs was resolute in his decision to return and save the company he had built.

A Personal Success Decision to Learn From

I have to be very careful here. I don't want to be the 1,000th book you read that provides endless inspirational examples like Steve Jobs and leaves you with the takeaway that you just have to be more like him. But we need to use examples to illustrate both how great decision-making can leave us in awe and provide a standard to aspire to. No matter how big and overwhelming your decision seems when you're in the middle of it, others have made similar decisions. Even if you're changing the world, others before you have done that too!

Learning from successful people is key. You'll notice that decisions in business in many ways parallel a combination of what you've set your sights on, strategy, and execution. We'll dive more into this later. So here's an example from a source a little less illustrious than Steve Jobs: that is me. But it's from my own personal experience and hence from my heart. As a marketing executive, I've had the opportunity to lead global marketing teams in technology and professional services companies. This means large teams and big budgets. But I've also had amazing opportunities to work at smaller entrepreneurial firms without the monster budgets and staff on hand. Both opportunities taught me tremendous lessons and contributed to my realization that a better approach to disciplined decision-making is needed.

I currently run marketing at a rapidly globalizing tech company called Teknicor. Teknicor is a global provider of data center core infrastructure, data protection, managed and cloud services. The company founders—Alan Fullerton and Mo Eisen—made a critical decision to set the company apart by always adopting best-of-breed technology, providing financial insights (often resulting in better technology at lower cost), and ensuring relentless execution to drive customer satisfaction. This is one of the most clearly focused visions I have seen in a company and it's built on a careful attention to culture. The thousands of decisions we make each year all align because of this clarity. Where most integrators would provide any technology the client asks for, Teknicor often challenges the client's own assumptions. We've literally turned away million-dollar deals when we felt the client was pushing for something that wasn't in their best interest and would eventually disappoint them. It has worked—the company has been growing triple digits and now spans three continents.

A Personal Failure Decision to Learn From

Beyond the corporate success stories I have shared here, like all of us, I have a number of failures that make for good learning scenarios. I'll share one that I think will resonate powerfully with smart career professionals. Very few people actually swing the bat large and fall hard. A far greater number of people are well-educated, well-paid professionals with great capabilities in their field of work—but with one thing missing. So many of these people, like me, want *more*. They want to make a lasting impact, beyond the routine of their everyday work.

Not what you envisioned as failure? It is—to many people. The disappointment that bears down on people in their search for passion brings with it a psychological cost. Like others, I found myself in this situation and dealt with it the way others do. I kept myself busy with projects, coming up with awesome ideas and executing some of them. I didn't lose a ton of money but didn't make a ton either. But because my sight lines weren't clear, I kept wandering, and the inevitable disappointment kept coming back. If this is how you feel occasionally, we'll discuss later how to uncover your personal passion.

Your Own Experience

Now we've read enough about the decisions of others. Take a moment to reflect on some of your own experience with the fresh lens of CE. Think back and identify both a huge success and a large failure. For each, write down a sentence to describe the situation, your decision, and the results. Also identify how clear you were on the long-term motivation if applicable, how tangible your targets were, and what actions you took. Take a moment to identify what barriers you faced and what you did about them (for the success and failure). Do you feel that any of these areas were lacking? Is there a possibility that this contributed to the success or failure you experienced? At this point, just jot down what you think overall. We'll take time later to revisit these personal decisions.

Do You Really Need This Book?

It's your business what you do with this book. Before you invest the time, I want you to be honest with yourself on why you're even contemplating reading it. If you're a business or organizational leader in a pretty good situation, wanting to improve your knowledge on decision-making, the book will certainly do that. If you're someone who hopes for a significantly different future, but isn't really feeling much pain in your current situation, it will likely help you improve your knowledge as well. Change, no matter which theory explains it, comes from within, not from a book. If you're not prepared to learn, and learn by taking action, you should ask for a refund. If you already have everything figured out (we know a lot of people who think they do) or think the world is against you, you should also ask for a refund.

This book will help you explore and understand what your personal vision may be and help you determine where your hunger lies—if you don't already feel it. As long as you're open minded and willing to put in some effort, I can help you. Before you make your decision on whether or not to proceed, ask yourself: What is the cost of not becoming a better decision maker? Do you feel a burning need for change? Decisions are the only way you can change. I hope to meet you at the next chapter!

THE CURRENT STATE OF DECISION THEORY

I f you're nerdy like me and actually enjoy the science behind the topic, then this section is for you. But no offense taken if you're too cool or want to get into action with game-changing decisions. Feel free to jump to the next section. Before we describe the main models, here's a quick summary:

Expected Utility	Behavioral Economics	Psychology	Causal Economics
A mathematically elegant model based on assumptions of 100 percent rational behavior. Proven wrong in the psychology lab. Limited to decisions that are one time period and don't involve a personal cost/benefit trade-off—just lottery outcomes that are either good or bad.	A mathematically elegant model that adds irrationality based on lab experiments. Limited to decisions that are one time period and don't involve a personal cost/benefit trade-off—just lottery outcomes that are either good or bad.	There are many powerful insights from psychology that can model and predict decision behavior; however, they usually apply to very specific lab-based scenarios and there is no unifying framework that can be utilized.	A mathematically robust model that incorporates rationality and irrationality through a cost and subsequent benefit trade-off over multiple time periods (causal coupling). Can model real decisions that involve upfront effort in pursuit of anticipated future rewards.

Current decision theories fall into a few major categories:

Rationality

This category includes classic economic decision theory, captured in expected utility and mainstream neoclassical economics. That's the economic approach used every day by the vast majority of people. It assumes that people are 100 percent rational.

Rationality and Irrationality

This category adds irrationality to the core rationality assumption. Applied psychology labs provide many insights into specific situations where irrationality comes into play. Behavioral Economics (BE) provides a very structured model that incorporates irrationality observations from the lab. At its core, BE provides tremendous insight into risk versus reward. For example, decision makers are motivated twice as much by avoiding risk than pursuing gain. Business management and government have implemented many insights from BE, especially in the area of nudging. Nudging suggests that better outcomes for society can result when public and private organizations affect the set of choices faced by agents to help them select the more beneficial ones. This aligns with the underlying idea of libertarian paternalism, which asserts that people can be influenced to make better decisions without taking away their fundamental right to make their own free choice. Nudging can underlie policies. For example, citizens may be defaulted into an organ donation program with the option to remove themselves at any time. Another example is schools placing healthy foods in a more convenient location than unhealthy ones.

Bounded rationality also fits in this category, capturing a "satisficing" approach based on the best available option, rational or not. It reflects limitations to our cognitive ability, and in combination with self-control challenges and ingrained social preferences, we can see significant irrational behavior. Psychology-based theories are typically situation-specific models, lacking in their ability to be formally and generally applied. Economics-based models typically contain formalized mathematical consistency, but oversimplify assumptions, making them impractical in application. Causal Economics incorporates rationality and irrationality.

Why Are We Irrational?
A lot is said about rationality versus irrationality. Irrationality can kick in when emotions take over calculating thoughts. When emotions are even-keeled, we're able to make rational decisions that are best for the long term. When emotional drivers kick into high gear, they serve as a kind of shorthand for making decisions. Emotions drive us quickly and powerfully, to decisively focus on what keeps us safe—and alive.

My reminder here is to never ever underestimate emotions. Emotions are more powerful than calculated thought. Calculated thoughts only mean something in the context of emotions and what those emotions mean to us personally. Emotions can run high and drive us quickly in one direction that may not be fully rational, and they can also support a lazy status quo. When people don't want to take action, it's not because it's illogical to do so. It's because they feel the emotional impact of having to move from their comfort zone. In his book *Predictably Irrational*,[1] famed behavioral economist Dan Ariely lays out why we behave in irrational ways in everyday life. With simple examples like drinking coffee, shedding pounds, buying a car, and selecting a mate, Ariely demonstrates that we consistently procrastinate, overpay, and underestimate when we make decisions. He also shows us why these misguided behaviors aren't random. They're systematic and predictable—predictably irrational. I highly recommend the book.

So What Is Economics?

The previous discussion on decision theory brings us back to the timeless question of "what is the science of economics?"

The classic answer of economists has usually been that economics is about the "allocation of scarce resources against unlimited demands." Then, the focus shifted to an "information economy" and information became the currency of interaction. In such a world, asymmetries in information between individuals and other challenges with the discovery and transmission of information became central.

Causal Economics (CE) brings us back even further to basics. Not that resources and information don't matter. They absolutely do. But, information and resource constraints are interpreted

---

1 Ariely, D. (2009). *Predictably Irrational, Revised and Expanded Edition: The Hidden Forces That Shape Our Decisions* (HarperCollins, London).

differently by individuals. At its core, economics is about individuals and the interaction of their incentives—first, their own personal preferences across cost and benefit, and then potential adjustments to those things as they interact with others and face external challenges to their initial cost and benefit calculations.

So in summary:

ECONOMICS ≠ RESOURCES
ECONOMICS ≠ INFORMATION
ECONOMICS = INCENTIVES

A very popular and easy-to-read book on Economics—*Super Freakonomics*[2]—contains this fundamental insight at its core. Incentives are everything. Information, resources, and so forth take shape in the context of incentives. Incentives are the very core of driving humans to do anything other than sit in inertia. *Super Freakonomics* is a great read of entertaining scenarios that show how our expectations can be turned upside down when we dig deep into how incentives drive people. CE shows us that these incentives formally come down to benefits we strive after and costs (certain and uncertain risks) that we avoid. If you think of economics and decision-making as the science of people and their incentives, you'll be light years ahead of others on the topic.

---

2 Dubner, S. J., and Levitt, S. D. (2010). *Superfreakonomics: Global Cooling, Patriotic Prostitutes and Why Suicide Bombers Should Buy Life Insurance* (Penguin Books, UK).

THE NEW FRONTIER: CAUSAL ECONOMICS

Finally a Realistic Model

Causal Economics (CE) is a new branch of Behavioral Economics (BE), which means it builds on the latter's basic structure. CE includes rationality and irrationality. It goes beyond the single period lottery (one single positive or negative) outcome approach of other models, capturing multiple time periods and deliberate costs incurred to produce expected future benefits. Sounds familiar? That's how real decisions are made. Formally, the concept is called "causal coupling." This multiple period structure includes causation between the vision we set our sights on, our targets, our actions, and our subsequent reactions.

In many ways, it's hard to imagine that for so long we've accepted decision-making models that cover only a single period and provide individuals with lottery-style outcomes—either win or loss. This is nothing like real-life decision-making. If you want to lose weight, your success isn't tied to a single day's decision about what to eat and how to work out. Moreover, the benefits of working out and following a healthy diet take more than a day to produce results. Success in losing weight involves a high-level, multi-period decision about diet and exercise, followed by a bunch of subsequent decisions. In addition, there's a very clear causation—working out and sacrificing junk food have to precede weight loss. Upfront costs leading to associated future benefits is the central idea behind *causal coupling*, which is the core formal insight of CE.

The bottom line is that most of the significant real-world decisions we face are like the example of losing weight. They take time and upfront, sustained efforts to produce results. Only CE is able to model these realistic decisions. Losing weight, starting a business, making an investment, building a relationship, and more. They all fit the bill. Individuals try to maximize their X (change in benefit/change in cost), and only decisions where X $\geq$ 1 makes sense.

What Are the Unique Insights of Causal Economics?

The most fundamental value of CE is that it provides a decision-making model that works in all cases—something that has been missing until now. But you're probably looking for an answer to the question "what are the big, new insights that are derived directly from CE?" In a nutshell, they are:

For business leaders, CE delivers new breakthrough ways to enhance your influence and ability to inspire others. It gets you better results.

For organizations, it provides a way to measure current decision-making competency and a method to improve it—resulting in a faster, more competitive organization that is better able to add value to customers and drive stronger profits.

For society, the CE approach produces sustainable economic and social policies that maximize fairness and benefits and minimize costs.

Causal Economics in a Word (Okay, Three Words)

"Freedom with Accountability"

This short and simple phrase succinctly captures the essence of CE from many angles. It means that the best outcomes ensure as much as possible that individuals have the freedom to decide how much personal total cost they are willing to bear for an expected personal total benefit. It's the simplest way to think of and remember the concept of causal coupling.

The CE perspective guides individuals to always be explicitly aware of the investment they are making and how it ties to target outcomes. It serves as a powerful personal improvement reminder—always be personally accountable for your own results, by investing cost (C) until you achieve target benefit (B). CE management means that leaders are constantly focused on understanding the complete costs their team faces and aligning benefits with these costs. It means that employees commit and act. In business, it generally means that talk is far down the value scale relative to action and tested reaction. It means clear sight and goals are prioritized over vague "listen to how smart people are" discussions. Companies are challenged to step up and reward results, not political posturing. CE places a laser focus on getting in deep to understand customer behaviors, not intent. "Camping out" (in the words of Stage-Gate founder, Dr. Cooper) and observing—not surveying—become the focus.[3]

Freedom with accountability extends beyond personal management and company management into social and political life. CE makes clear that the only government policies that are truly fair, effective, and sustainable are those that causally couple B and C

---

3 Robert G. Cooper, Scott J. Edgett and Elko J. Kleinschmidt (2002) "Optimizing the Stage-Gate Process: What Best-Practice Companies Do—I." *Research-Technology Management*, 45(5), 21–27. DOI: 10.1080/08956308.2002.11671518

across citizens. This means that each individual is able to benefit from their contributions through free exchange and are obligated to bear their share of societal costs and any externalities generated through their private activities.

Are these all new ideas? No. The core ideas of CE are new, but many of the implications for leadership and other aspects reinforce well-known concepts that you're likely familiar with. The goal of CE is to provide a consistent and pragmatic model that works. If you approach all of your thinking with CE in mind, I truly believe that your self-management, leadership, and societal impact will improve.

If You Remember Only Four Things from This Book... What Should They Be?

The following are four key takeaways from this book, each of which are discussed subsequently.

1. **Causal Coupling (Incentives):** Understand that incentives (costs and benefits) drive all behavior and that decisions cannot be modelled with traditional neoclassical economics and BE—outcomes are not random, whether rational or not; they require upfront cost (deliberate and risk) followed by anticipated benefit, which is the principle of "causal coupling" at the core of CE. People only pursue options where they personally expect $X \geq 1$ (i.e., causal coupling is achieved).

2. **STAR (Management Framework):** Make your decisions explicitly within the STAR framework (Sights, Targets, Actions, Reactions). It covers end-to-end focus and execution.

3. **Change Ratio (Change Management):** Always know your change ratio—CODN/BODS (cost of doing nothing/benefit of doing something)—and that of others. No change occurs until this threshold is hit.

4. **X ≥ 1 (Sustainability):** Ensure all your decisions provide X ≥ 1 (i.e., causal coupling is achieved) for all key stakeholders; otherwise people will have the incentive to undermine the decisions.

Causal Coupling

Freedom with accountability is a practical way of capturing the core theoretical foundation of CE—formally known as causal coupling. Whenever you think about CE, keep the concept of causal coupling front and center in your mind and you'll have clarity to apply the model. Causal coupling means that individuals always face costs (deliberate and risk) before benefits (anticipated) when making decisions. This is individual-level causal coupling. In general, the world does not provide free lunches, and even when costs are not explicit, decision makers face opportunity costs. Causal coupling exists for a decision maker whenever X (change in B/change in C) ≥ 1 for the decision maker over the time horizon relevant to the decision.

Causal coupling also extends to interactions between individuals, in markets, through government policy, and other areas of society. Such interactions are as fair and sustainable as possible when costs and benefits are causally coupled for most individuals. This means people are freely rewarded for the contributions they make, but on the flip side they aren't able to continuously free ride on the contributions of others at a significant level. Causal coupling across society exists whenever X (change in B/change in C) ≥ 1 for the majority of people involved or impacted over the time horizon relevant to the decision.

If you keep the principle of causal coupling in mind at all times, you'll be able to anticipate the vast majority of implications of individual decisions and social policies. For a more in-depth and technical look at the economic theory, feel free to visit CausalEconomics. com, after completing this book and getting into action.

The STAR Framework

Let's return to a very direct look at powerful individual decision-making. This is what matters most to managers. The STAR (**S**ights, **T**argets, **A**ctions, **R**eactions) framework is a powerful way for individuals to define their decisions. It captures the focus and sustained action elements of effective decision-making. Decisions are still ultimately made such that an individual's $X \geq 1$. The STAR framework further maps out the structure of such decisions.

The B/C and STAR elements align as follows:

$$ST \,/\, AR = B \,/\, C$$

This implies that benefit is for the most part captured in the sights and targets we set. People generally set sights and targets that reflect states of extensive benefit, not costs. For example, a chef would set his or her sights on making great tasting food and aim to open a restaurant that delivered this, as opposed to making horrible tasting food and opening a restaurant that delivered poor taste. It sounds obvious, but for the sake of complete clarity we will make this point. On a similar note, the actions and reactions we have to take on generally reflect the cost and effort stages we face in order to achieve our S and T. So, we end up with the parallel $ST \,/\, AR = B \,/\, C$. Another helpful way of understanding and remembering STAR is to think of the following natural flow:

S & T = Focus
A & R = Execution

The STAR framework is also easy to remember because it's a common acronym and it can literally be drawn as a star diagram that flows clockwise.

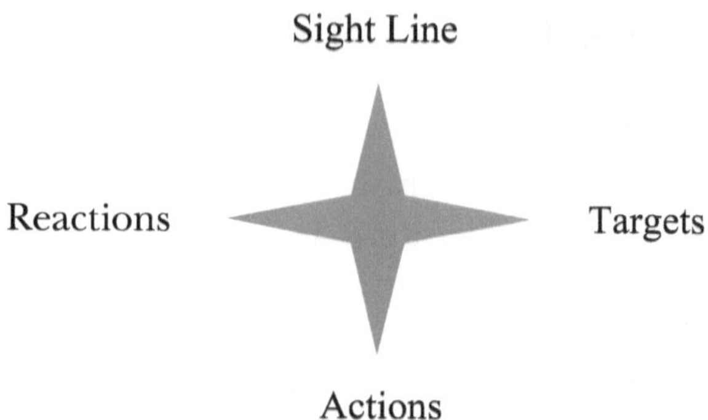

How Do You Know You'll Follow Through? The Change Ratio

With all the techniques just discussed, how do you know that you'll actually change? Each one of us has dropped the ball on a decision. It's human nature. One measure makes all the difference, and if you can use your judgment to quantify this one measure, you'll have a pretty good idea as to whether a particular decision will stick.

The measure is CODN/BODS.

This is the ratio of the cost of doing nothing (CODN) to the benefit of doing something (BODS). Every single person will only make decisions that stick when this ratio is sufficiently high for them. As the ratio increases, the pain of not changing rises and we find it less painful to take action. Hence, people in dire situations can successfully drive change. Poverty, reputation, and other factors can create this pain of the status quo.

Let me be absolutely clear. We ONLY change in a sustainable way when our CODN/BODS ratio hits our "that's enough" level.

Sustainability—Is It Really as Easy as X ≥ 1?

I know. It's audacious to suggest that to a large degree the optimality and sustainability of decisions can be judged by one simple formula: $X \geq 1$ (reflecting causal coupling). But I stand behind it. This simple formula is so powerful that it can be applied to personal decisions, business strategies, political policies, and anything else that involves decisions by people and between people.

As an individual decision maker, you need to incorporate all elements of cost and benefit—rational and irrational. And you'll have sustainable success if you find ways to make sure others you depend on for implementation also face a benefit to cost ratio $X \geq 1$ in your desired scenarios.

This is critical because so few people genuinely invest time in understanding the perspective of others on whom they depend. Focusing on the explicit X ratio of others builds this into the process and delivers results that are sustainable for everyone. In everyday language, causal coupling means that you benefit more than you lose and that others benefit or at least don't lose.

$X \geq 1$ is a convenient shorthand for the very simple principle that everyone involved in any interaction should benefit more than the cost they face. It means a win-win for everyone involved/impacted.

Everyday Examples

This book introduces a significant new theory grounded in academic research and formal mathematical modelling. It provides the necessary foundation that ensures consistent application and interpretation of results. But that's no excuse to not present examples that demonstrate the importance of the CE perspective in your management style.

Losing Weight

A classic and easy-to-understand example that drives home how CE accurately captures real-world decisions where other models don't, is that of losing weight. Most of us can relate to a weight loss goal. Most of us have probably been on this journey personally. Well, I know I have. A weight loss target is a great example because it's perfectly modelled by CE and can't be effectively modelled by mainstream economics, including traditional BE. That's because the decision to lose weight is multi-period—it's not just one trip to the gym or one pass on the box of donuts in the office. It's not a lottery of either weight loss or weight gain of various amounts. It's deliberate upfront effort in the form of workouts and dieting willpower, day in and day out, with direct causation to weight loss results as a result of the effort. It is tough to put in the upfront effort, but it is fully deterministic. There is essentially no luck involved. If the effort is put in and the sacrifices made, the results will come. It's hard to find a stronger example where we can fully control our destiny. The exact amount of time required to hit a target may be slightly variable, but the target is fully within each person's control.

That doesn't make it easy. It just illustrates that the CE model captures this type of decision, whereas other models that cover just a single period and produce random, lottery-style outcomes of either gain or loss cannot even capture the scenario parameters, let alone explain them.

Starting a Business

Starting a business shares similarities with our weight loss example, but also a number of critical differences. With a weight loss target, an individual can control almost all inputs, even though they are faced with many external temptations. You can go to the gym. You can decide specifically what to eat. Starting a business reflects a hierarchy of decisions. There is the deep reflection decision that starting a business is good for you, despite the inevitable costs and risks. There are then many subsequent decisions regarding whether to stay on course or make a diversion.

Starting and building a business brings into play many more influences that are beyond the decision maker's control. Unlike showing up to a gym that is going to be there for you, your competitors are actively trying to win at your expense. Anyone who has started a business knows that it requires massive effort upfront. Effort implies work, risks, sacrifices, and more—all high personal costs. Hence, there's anticipation of large benefits in terms of future flexibility and wealth. Financial freedom and stability in this case are hard won as a result. The CE decision model captures this reality perfectly with extended time horizons, significant upfront effort, and delayed benefit. It's almost offensive for entrepreneurs to try to model this type of decision with the traditional rational economic expected utility theory.

Traditionally, psychology defines *risk* as a "downside," whereas economics defines it as volatility. CE defines risk mathematically as potential cost, along the lines of psychology. Clearly the risk in business is that of loss, not volatility. Volatility that produces massive upside gains would be welcomed by most entrepreneurs I know! This clarifies the silliness of some of the assumptions in mainstream economic decision-making theory, made for the purpose of relative mathematical simplicity. Whether you're an entrepreneur or a loved one is, when all of you have a CE perspective on decision-making, you can maximize clarity—maximizing B/C as much as possible in the long term.

Investing

Another great example to drive home why we need CE to improve our decision-making is the classic example of securities markets. This is the bastion of economic rationality. The Capital Asset Pricing Model (CAPM) is the flagship rational equilibrium model that demonstrates how market decision-making is purported to work. Most of us are aware of how far from the truth this is. Emotion is rampant in trading and investing—we have perhaps experienced it (I worked as a stock trader, so I know I have). Many people irrationally jump in on the hype late in the game, following which shrewd investors exit, creating a run-down and maybe even a crash. Professional economists too know that CAPM doesn't work.

It creates supposedly precise pricing values for assets, but these are meaningless because they're based on unrealistic assumptions.

The problem is that no other models are as mathematically easy to use here. For example, CE explains the rational/irrational combined behavior seen in the markets, with boom/bust cycles making perfect sense. CE also provides very precise mathematical formulae for individual decision-making. However, it doesn't impose unrealistic assumptions to create equilibriums. It leaves open a whole barrage of solutions. That's where it is less exciting to some professional economists. But this lack of a small set of equilibrium solutions doesn't mean that CE doesn't allow effective predications. It's quite the opposite. By observing C and B ranges that decision makers face, it is possible to forecast with CE in a way not possible with traditional economics.

Dating

For those of you who are tired of all typical business examples, let's take a look at the softer side of life. Love and dating. Let's just say it has been a while since I learned anything about dating. Is it the softer side of life? I hear it's a jungle out there. So maybe this isn't as happy an example as I'd hoped. Regardless, dating provides a great example of where CE allows us to explain and anticipate decisions better than other theories.

Every human on the planet needs to selfishly take care of their own core needs for survival, family, and prosperity. This selfishness isn't a bad thing. Once a person is able to reasonably secure the future of their family, they can comfortably begin to think about the needs of others. When seeking a mate, it's reasonable that one takes care of their own affairs and finds another that values it and likewise takes care of their own affairs. This all comes down to each person thinking long term about their own investments in life and what they expect in return. CE captures this long-term, mutually selfish, and altruistic perspective.

Buying Junk Food on the Spot

Not every decision in life is as overwhelming as the examples we just explored. Sometimes we may find ourselves facing temptation at the checkout counter, as a decadent bar of chocolate stares back at us. This is certainly not a rational decision, which comes down to supply and demand. Few people make a calculated decision to go shopping for chocolate and then go to the store to look at pricing and make a quantity decision.

This example aligns well with all the current buzz around "nudging" (based on the work of Nobel economist Richard Thaler). The chocolate bars could have been placed anywhere in the store, but because they are an impulse buy, they're near the checkout counters. In this case, the rigorous modelling of nudging in BE is a formalization of what marketers have been doing for some time.

So how do we model this decision? It's a single-period decision, so could mainstream economics or BE shed some light? It's certainly not a rational calculation. The cost is trivial and the quantity pretty static. You might buy one or two, but you're not analyzing this economically. It's a straight-up yummy, emotional decision. BE provides considerable insight into our experience. It's an example of nudging and of psychological framing.

These elements of BE are really just taken from psychology. The core insight of BE—that risk and reward are perceived differently and that they differ depending on where they are relative to the status quo—doesn't really apply here. Buying a chocolate bar isn't high risk... or is it?

It all depends on the decision maker. Each of us has a very different set of beliefs that provides a frame for how we interpret B and C. So if the decision maker is a health buff, they will see the chocolate bar as a big cost/risk in terms of added belly flab. More importantly, they see a small transgression against their beliefs as a potential floodgate to ongoing breaches—costs that exceed the sacrifice of not indulging. They will see resisting the chocolate bar as an example of their resolve and success—benefits that exceed the cost of forgoing great taste.

Resolutions

If the examples I shared so far haven't resonated with you personally, the good old New Year's resolution example should hit home. We're all inundated with this concept every year-end. In my experience, there are four ways people usually handle these, which is illustrative of how perspective entirely frames a decision. Here are some examples:

1. Person #1: This person avoids making resolutions, claiming that it's too hyped up. Yes, a lot of it is hyped, but this as an easy excuse that many people use. Timing isn't an issue; results are. Just because other people may come up empty on their resolutions does not mean others should not be making/following up on their own resolutions. Such people are usually looking for a way to *not* commit to goals and not feel bad doing so. They don't move forward. They enjoy B from feeling good about their position of criticizing others and face no C because they don't have to do anything.

2. Person #2: This person gets completely excited, setting unrealistic goals with no eye on the realities of executing them. A useless exercise, this kind of goal setting usually leads to the next example. Such people are emotional and often defensive, so friends and family just shut up and let them do their thing. They usually enjoy B from running all the ideas in their head—which is fun and inspiring. And they move on so quickly to the next resolution or distraction that they don't take on any mental C.

3. Person #3: This person has been a #2 in the past and now does not trust him or herself to do it again. This is basically a way of letting past defeats reduce chances for future success.

Such people do not get B from setting their sights on any exciting outcomes. They also carry a general overhanging C from the "depression" of feeling defeated and not finding many opportunities.

4. Person #4: This person treats this as a great time to assess as they do on a regular basis. What others do doesn't matter. They will usually review their STAR on a quarterly or frequent basis. They are more likely, as a result of taking ownership of their destiny, to experience more C and even more B.

So, New Year's resolutions aren't good or bad. How you approach them is good or bad, just like we would look at decisions on any other day of the year. Because we have personal experiences with resolutions, they're a great example to understand the different ways people can make decisions based on their C and B perceptions.

Famous Examples

We can learn from both successes and failures, but more so from failures. Let's get inspired by looking at some of the most famous horrible business decisions and feel good that we didn't make them! Here are some examples.

Blockbuster Video

If you're my age, you'll remember physically going to a store to get a VHS and/or DVD to watch a movie at home. Blockbuster video was the king of the business. They were literally on every corner. In the nineties, they had almost 10,000 stores and roughly $6 billion annual revenue. A little start-up called Netflix offered them $50 million at the turn of the millennium to help them launch their new DVD-by-mail service. Blockbuster said no. Try and find a Blockbuster Video now. Netflix is now valued at more than $150 billion. So what went wrong? Management was compensated for short-term results, not long-term impact, so the professional management actually came out ahead, making their salaries and bonuses for a few years without rocking the boat with risk. This is a common environment for corporate managers who do not have significant equity.

It's an example of decoupled cost and benefit and the resulting misaligned incentives. It doesn't make sense for most corporate managers to swing the bat on industry redefining trends because it just adds career risk and no committed upside. Even though Blockbuster is a famous example, it is so just because of how quickly the business model changed and amplified the decoupling. The decision itself is quite common across many businesses—professional non-ownership management does better under the status quo than they can expect to, under massive upheaval change. Industry change is the domain of entrepreneurs with incentives aligned to swinging the bat and shaking up the establishment.

Motorola
So what do you think? Is the smartphone a thing? No doubt it is. If you don't have a smartphone, you are out of step with the world. Sorry. They're that ubiquitous. Do you remember the popular Razr mobile phone that Motorola put on the market? It was a big part of the reason that Motorola achieved a huge 22 percent market share in the mid-2000s. But the company didn't take the shift to smartphones seriously. They launched one, but they did it slowly, without urgency. It was 2010 before they got one to market—very late in the game! At one point, the giant's market value dropped over 80 percent. As we'll touch on many times in this book, "speed" is absolutely critical in all effective decision-making. If you're moving slowly, competitors will move past you. Motorola could easily have made smaller, faster decisions if it was truly concerned about risk. For an organization this size though, risk isn't the issue. The inertia comes down to incentives again. The leadership thought they would come out ahead by maintaining the status quo as long as

they could. This means that their fortunes weren't aligned to the changing scenarios. They saw low risk and high reward for doing little and high risk and low reward for making big changes. The management and the board both focused on short-term outcomes instead of the long-term industry.

As noted earlier, this is a common approach for large companies to structure incentives. It's also the reason that innovation almost always comes from smaller companies. A huge insight is the realization that the stereotype that smaller companies are more innovative because they can move quickly is true, but only part of the story. What's really behind this is the reality that the incentive structure at smaller companies is more aligned with innovation. This translates to equity sitting with the current owners and key talent, rather than being spread out in small chunks across the broad public of relatively passive investors.

Yahoo

We all know Yahoo and Microsoft. But not all of us know that Yahoo could have sold to Microsoft but turned down the offer and went into continued decline afterward. In 2000, Yahoo was worth roughly $125 billion, but was already in visible decline. In 2008, Yahoo's founder turned down an offer of roughly $45 billion and continued to see a decline to the low $20 billion range. It's still not a small number, but it's a big erosion of value. What went wrong? Here's a surprising example where a founder with equity made emotional decisions that flew in the face of rationality. He saw the cost of admitting failure as higher than that of the actual financial costs that ensued. He attached more benefit to being seen as "right" than to actual higher financial returns.

Ford

After a few disappointing failures, let's conclude with a positive example. Henry Ford is one of the biggest business icons of all times. Everyone sees him as the king of the industrial revolution—all about machinery, not people. But one of the biggest innovations Henry Ford made concerned people and a deep appreciation of causal coupling. He doubled his workers' wages. This was essentially the first time in history that employees were seen as an investment, not just an expense to be minimized. This cost Ford more money in the short term, but lowered costs and generated higher productivity in the long term. Because workers and the company were clearly aligned. This decision was massively against prevailing wisdom at the time and it left its mark on corporate culture even up to the current times.

Examples from Your Experience

It's an absolutely great idea to learn from others' experiences, but it's just as important to look back at your own experiences as learning opportunities. Take a moment now to write down the biggest success you recall and the biggest failure you recall. Map out the elements of STAR for each as you recall them at the time. Did you find that your biggest success had better depth and alignment across the STAR elements?

CAUSAL ECONOMICS DECISION FOUNDATIONS

A Decision Is Only as Good as Its Context

The field of psychology offers accurate lab-tested insights that explain every conceivable behavior in some way. The challenge with psychology as an academic discipline is that it lacks anything even close to a unifying theory or model that people can apply. Economics, on the other hand, adopts this unifying model approach but traditionally has unrealistic assumptions that make these models equally difficult to apply. That's why BE has taken off so strongly. It maintains the disciplined modelling of economics and formally infuses psychological factors.

Big Decisions. Little Decisions.

Some astute readers are going to point out that the four-element STAR model seems like a lot to think about when trying to make decisions in today's fast-paced world. Does this model make sense when someone is looking to buy a pop at a variety store? Well, it does and it doesn't. All decisions, big or small, do involve the model. Smaller decisions just check the boxes a lot faster, taking certain elements as given. For example, when deciding to lose weight, one does soul searching around the outcome they set their sights on—how they want to look and feel. It takes time to entrench a new vision. Unlike flippant New Year's resolutions, truly setting a *sight* with emotion that one can feel, see, and articulate, is a big step. With that in place, *targets*, *actions*, and *reactions* fall in line. Things like serious weight loss, business ventures, and so on, require upfront sight-setting, or they will fail.

Small decisions, like what kind of pop to buy at the counter, will for the most part fit into other decisions you have made about how you view the world. You might not realize it, but you have made a decision on pop already, consistent with your vision. Some people place health so high as an objective, they will avoid pop. Some value spontaneously "treating themselves" and will grab a cold pop on a hot day when they see it. Some people have a sight line that money should be spent frugally, which means they'll avoid all these little transactions that "add up."

Whether we like it or not, we're constantly guided by our dominant decisions about what sight(s) we envision as important. Personal performance guru Anthony Robbins refers to these as values. They're things we have agreed to, either by owning our destiny or taking the views of others. How you view money, fun, and relationships defines a core set of decisions about how you view the world, based on these particular views. So without any resetting of your decisions about how you view the world, your small decisions like buying soda pop will fall in line with bigger decisions you've already made. That is, they follow the sight and targets—or lack of targets—you have set for yourself. Therefore, making a major life change involves changing a core set of decisions about the world, and everything else follows.

Perspective Is Everything

Your perspective is 100 percent your choice. If you don't believe this, it's critical that you stop here and reflect. We all perceive the world through our senses. We interpret external influences through our own way of seeing the world. Imagine a $200,000 sports car—a Lamborghini for example. Cars are not your thing? Cool. Maybe a $5 million home? If these are not a big deal for you, pick your own example of something that's currently out of your financial reach.

When presented with your chosen "out of reach" goal, what do you do? Some people will decide that it's unachievable due to their current budget and try to forget it. Some people will decide they're going to acquire the target item, and to do so must find a way to make more money. Others may come up with creative ways to access it, without the full spend of a purchase—for example, renting it, time sharing it, and so on. The outside world only provides situations that are the result of many people's previous decisions. Decision makers can accept the world, or change it.

Your perspective is how you frame the world. It's how you attach costs and benefits to various alternative scenarios. Framing is just what it sounds like—boundaries applied to the way a situation is viewed. Either you apply your own framing or others will be happy to do it for you—to their advantage. Values and beliefs are your internal gauge by which you judge incoming stimuli. Vegans, omnivores, and carnivores have very different perceptions about eating meat, fully defined by their values and beliefs.

The truly scary thing is that many people didn't explicitly choose their values and beliefs. In most cases, they inherited them from the outside world, believing what they were told to believe. Few people would admit it, but it's rare that someone actually sits down and determines their own beliefs and values. Values and beliefs generally get further entrenched over time, as new information is evaluated with selective perception and results in confirmation bias. Selective perception and confirmation biases imply that we give more weight to information that aligns with what we already believe and value. Status quo bias reminds us that change always includes perceived discomfort costs, which makes the status quo seem relatively attractive. It underpins decision-making inertia.

There are several additional psychological principles that further determine how we end up perceiving things. Anchoring and compartmentalizing are major elements of framing. Marketers and political influencers put a lot of effort into anchoring our attention by using specific cues, like numbers and words. Compartmentalizing is something we do in order to boil many complex options down into a manageable number of categories. Distinction bias is another element of framing where decision makers are able to distinguish between alternatives when they are placed side by side. The recency principle demonstrates that decision makers give more weight to the most recent things they experience, over which they have better recognition.

I started this section by saying that your perspective is 100 percent your choice. It is in the present and into the future. But don't for a second forget that you, me, and every one of us have been shaped by what others have told us all our lives. From childhood to adulthood, we're bombarded with all kinds of agendas! Objective facts are almost nonexistent in the human world. Everything is interpreted to give it meaning. Good or bad, our beliefs are heavily built up by others. That's why no other role is more important than that of a parent and the influences that a child is presented with. No matter how smart you are and how much you've figured the world out, you're one among billions of people and you have been influenced by the beliefs of others. No matter where your head is at now, from this point on you can fully direct it *if* you master decision-making. Master decision-making and you master your destiny. There's nothing more positive than that!

Step Outside Yourself

We know how powerful our emotions are and how they drive our bias. But how do we get around our own perspectives even when we know they're biased? We have to find a way to look in from outside our own mind. It takes practice to reset our view to the bigger picture. To illustrate, consider an "out there" example of drastically changing the viewpoint from yourself to *outside* of yourself. Imagine yourself on a beautiful summer day in a field of flowers and grass, surrounded by trees, a nice breeze, and summer scents. Now let's turn that whole image around by changing the perspective. The perspective we described reflects the view of a human being at the top of the food chain in a wealthy country. Consider it this way though. What you see around you is beautiful because you are in the position you are. The world around you is actually a war zone of insects and animals eating living plants and each other for survival. This is happening every minute of every day, but it's out of your vision. It doesn't directly hurt you. Nothing changed the environment, but by seeing the situation from a view larger than ourselves, we go from seeing paradise to seeing a much crueler world.

Focus Drives Everything

The famous expression "you get what you measure" is true. That's why targets are so critical. Targets focus your mind, which frames your perspective and prioritizes that direction. Tony Robbins demonstrates this using a classic example. He asks students to look around the room and notice all of the people wearing brown in the room. After they're done, he asks how much red they saw. Everyone is stumped because they were so focused on observing brown and hence ignored red due to the instructions. This is a very simple example of *priming.* Priming puts us into a particular target mindset. Marketers and salespeople use priming to its fullest!

Many people are conditioned to believe that they need to love everything they do. This attitude sounds appealing, but it's a major reason for failure. In pursuing ambitious targets, we often get uncomfortable, and we need to. If we're driven by results, there will be plenty of painful things we have to do each day on our journey. Tony Robbins jumps into ice cold water every morning. He definitely doesn't want to do it, but it displays a mental conditioning that puts him in the right mental state. So often we focus on fear as the only barrier to change. In my experience that's rarely the main barrier. Most people aren't happy with their decision-making because they haven't sufficiently defined a passionate vision/line of sight.

But Focus Isn't Real without Passion

Not to take away from the previous section, but we've seen many examples of people who focus on something, but that focus isn't aligned with passion. Focus cannot be purely logical. It has to be viscerally embedded in your soul for it to matter. People don't do anything that isn't super important to them emotionally. If that emotion is backed by rationality, then you're certainly on the right path. This is the reason we spend so much time emphasizing that you need to uncover passion first and then turn that into a focus. You can't go the other way around, and this critical insight doesn't get enough attention. Think back to your childhood. As a kid, the things you got excited about were the things you just tried and felt a passion for. Do the same thing as an adult. Find your passions by trying and doing things, not by analyzing and thinking after reading books like this. A book like this can help in tightening focus in areas where your passion exists or areas that need exploration. As long as you're being honest with yourself, it's also pretty likely that you know what your core passions are. If you are "established"—okay "older"!—there's a really good chance you have a great idea of your passion areas.

How Do You Get a Super Passionate Sight Line?

Have you heard the clichéd advice to just get uncomfortable? There is good intent in this statement, but on its own it's naive. No one has the motivation to become uncomfortable. We move away from discomfort, toward comfort. What differs is how individuals define these things. Many people find considerable comfort in the status quo and see a lot of discomfort in new situations. These people don't seem to do too much to push themselves. Why should they? But other individuals see lots of discomfort in the status quo and relatively more comfort in new situations. Once pain in the status quo exceeds a threshold, people embrace change. This threshold is captured in a simple ratio; the CODN (cost of doing nothing)/BODS (benefit of doing something). Unless your sights are aligned with beliefs that associate massive pain with the status quo, you won't truly pursue change. That's reality.

Overcoming Fear

Fear is natural. We would not want to live without fear. Fear protects us. But we can manage when it is applied. Fear applied to really dangerous things is great. It protects us from diving out of a plane without a parachute. Things like this should genuinely scare the crap out of us, but many things we fear in our lives are situations where we blow impact and probability out of proportion. Fear directly results from our perception of the size and probability of potential damage. For example, few of us have a fear of tying our shoelaces—we've done it thousands of times and we don't see a real downside. But something like public speaking scares many people. It makes us worry about looking silly in front of our peers.

So, what's the best way to get around our paralyzing fears? It's to condition ourselves to act in the face of it, focusing not on the fearful situation, but instead on the replacement activities that keep us fully committed to taking action. Over time, the old fear will become familiar and comfortable!

Cost and Risks

A massive insight from CE is a deep understanding of cost and risk. In traditional economic theory, risk is equated with variance. But that doesn't make sense because variation includes upside benefit and downside risk. Psychology traditionally sees risk in this proper duality and that's the perspective utilized in CE. Costs can either be current or certain to occur in the future (via contracts, etc.). Risks are future based; they're costs that could occur in the future. Different people react differently to certain costs and risks. To make decisions with the most clarity, always keep in mind the important distinction between cost and risk.

Neuro Associations

Personal cost and benefit aren't only perceived mental associations. They are also literally biologically ingrained through nervous system dynamics. Whenever a large emotion is attached to a certain situation, it gets etched into our nervous system through neural pathways. That's why we remember experiences that were highly emotional. And that's also why we don't remember every mundane experience. Understanding this allows us to realize that we can indeed manage our physiological/mental associations by managing our perceptions. We associate pain with undesirable outcomes and pleasure with target outcomes. As we continuously practice and do so in an emotional context, our associations will become deeply ingrained.

Self-Talk

A technique that doesn't get enough attention in my opinion is that of self-talk. I'll go as far as saying that if you aren't engaging in self-talk, you're not in full control, and definitely not in your superconscious state (something we will discuss later). Self-talk sets the actual rhythm of your thoughts, keeping you in proactive thinking mode. Self-talk works hand-in-hand with questions, visualization, and interruptions. Silent self-talk is better than nothing, but if you're able to, engaging in out loud self-talk is the most powerful.

Interrupts

If you've ever embarked on any type of self-help program, you may be among many people who found it tremendously challenging to get out of your habitual grind in order to instill new behaviors. This is one of the biggest challenge areas. When we have a comfortable status quo, like many of us do, interrupting our flow is very tough. How do we do it? Many experts focus on little tricks to shake up behaviors and jolt routines. These are needed, but we have to start at the most fundamental level to ensure lasting change. Not surprisingly this means we need to first look at what we've set our sights on.

I can't stress enough how important "interruptions" are. We all lead such constantly busy lives today that we fall into a cadence of reacting to the endless barrage of external stimuli. In these conditions, the situation reinforces itself. Please don't think I'm making an unrealistic assertion that you need to stay 100 percent focused and avoid all distractions and interruptions to your targets. In the real world, interruptions sometimes have to be addressed. For example, a client may have an urgent and unexpected need that you have to deal with, temporarily sidelining your planned activities. Family emergencies are going to happen. If you have a day job, your employer is going to throw urgent deadlines at you. This is reality. You can't avoid all distractions. You need to be alert to when they happen and manage them to stay the course. There's only one way to do that. Learning to interrupt your own autopilot behaviors. You need to learn how to jolt yourself from subconscious and conscious states to your superconscious mental state.

Questions

I believe decisions are the engine that drives all progress. But if I had to pick other concepts that were right up there in importance, I would choose "questions," which help us generate alternatives and seek trusted external insights. Without questions, we think in autopilot, reacting to stimuli the way we are conditioned to. This is the opposite of an environment that supports change. It reinforces status quo.

Questions are the tool that guides the mind. Without a language we can't think in advanced terms, as everything remains poorly defined. Without questions, language isn't directed and we aren't in control. Questions are how we uncover and assign pain and pleasure to things. Actions are what entrench them. Questioning shakes that up. They jolt the conscious mind and even the subconscious mind into new directions. An even better step is turning your questions into self-talk. You can do it quietly! Taking this approach lets you direct and expand your thinking in powerful new directions.

Visualization

Most of us are aware of the power of visualization. With visualization, we place ourselves into our desired situation so we can "experience" it. By picturing ourselves in our desired outcome state and associating major benefits with it, we condition our mind to hunger for it. Similarly, by picturing our current status quo and attaching pain to it, we bring visceral emotions into play because sight is a very powerful sense.

All of Our Senses

One of the challenges of visualization is that our optical sense can take in so many stimuli. It can create so much complexity that the direct connection to root emotions can be weakened. Hearing, smell, touch, and taste are simpler; they pick up on less elements in each stimulus. Hence, they more often directly tie to powerful emotions. Think of how you feel when your favorite song comes on. You almost always get a pretty direct emotional boost. No complex interpretation is required like a visual mental photograph.

You simply feel pumped and your physiology and state follow suit. The direct and simple emotional link is illustrated by the usually binary response. You hear a song. You either like it and feel great or you don't. Same with the taste of a dish. It's a pretty simple connection. Same with the scents we smell. For these reasons, you shouldn't only rely on the popular technique of visualization. Add it to all the other ones.

As always, there's a caveat. Don't just rely on other senses and omit visualization. That's because the direct and simple emotional connection of these other senses also keeps them pretty tied to the current time period. It is harder to connect a smell so vividly to a future state you want to arrive at. Visualization lets you fill in specifics, like the particular dream car you want to drive. Be careful, because these less articulated senses can lull you into an emotion but not direct it. Think of playing your music and just enjoying it, without it driving you to specific thoughts. Music in particular is very rhythmic and can easily do this. So you have to practice how you use music. Feel the emotion as you tie it to visual and other sensory associations. The bottom line is to always use multiple senses and always include visualization.

Analyze

For good reason we've been focusing intently on the point of decision and execution. This is where most people need to improve their approach. But we have to step back and consider the serious analysis that should precede decisions whenever possible. Analysis really comes down to a few core activities:

- Data collection
- Criteria definition (sight, targets)
- Generating alternatives and associating B/C trade-offs for each

A book on analysis is probably a lot less exciting for leaders than one on decisions, but I want to ensure you take this concept seriously. Data collection is a dangerous activity. It can lead to the classic analysis paralysis if overdone and to poor decisions if material data is missed.

More Information Is Almost Never the Answer

I'm in the information business, but I'll be the first to tell you that information is far less important than we all believe. Information and education are almost always served as the answer to problems, but they are rarely what is needed. Public awareness campaigns, corporate initiatives, and so forth center on providing information through orchestrated messages. Organizations repeat this process of "educating" over and over again, but it usually serves as nothing more than a check box against supposed due diligence.

Information can help people move toward a decision efficiently, but it has NOTHING to do with incentives—either on the cost or benefit side. I also work in IT, and it frustrates me that we see the world only as an information economy. Yes, that is the dominant industry space, just like agriculture and manufacturing used to be. But information and data are not the currency of success. Most of the data out there are cluttered and duplicated. We are in a decision economy, and in fact that is the core of all economies. Sorry that it makes for less trendy discussions, but it's the truth.

Where information does really make a difference is when it comes from someone who's taken action and is sharing practical nuances they learned in the reaction stage of their own decisions that helped them arrive at success. Most other information is usually devoid of the real-world context necessary for effective implementation. I will go as far to say that you should always discount the advice of those who have not obtained the end state you are striving for.

A major chunk of our business landscape recycles obvious information. Ideas and information pertaining to leadership, teamwork, financial analysis, and so forth are not mysterious. They take effort to implement. I am not saying this to be negative or critical. I want to ensure that you realize how much of the knowledge out there is a waste of time. It's simple. Stop seeking new insights or information—instead, role model others and take small actions. This is the best way to align your hard work with successful results.

Think of the last time you saw a "leader" issue a mandate. Was it a rah-rah sharing of information and call for action, not directly tied to any targets or actions—and definitely not something they followed up on to help their team through the reaction stages? In other words, a great many "leadership" decisions are simply vague edicts. They are destined to fail, and unfortunately many managers know this; they know they won't be held accountable for results on many of their decisions. So they play the game, barking out orders and claiming the quality of their team isn't where it needs to be.

Speed Is Absolutely Vital

Comprehensive research by Elena Botelho, published in *Harvard Business Review*,[4] provides incredible insight on decision-making by CEOs. On studying CEOs from all backgrounds (Ivy League and otherwise) and company sizes, the insight that came to the forefront was that great speed is associated with great decision makers. These leaders make good decisions, move, obtain feedback, and course-correct, as opposed to over-analyzing and letting information get old. Aging of information aside, we always have to make decisions with much less information than desired. CEOs in particular have to be confident in making decisions quickly, because they set the pace for their company and employees. This is one of the biggest takeaways you can apply to your own decision-making

---

4 Botelho, E. L., Powell, R. K., Kincaid, S., and Wang, D. (2017). "What Sets Successful CEOs Apart." *Harvard Business Review*, 95(3), 70–77.

as you practice. Make decisions that balance your benefit and cost trade-off goals and move on to the next one.

A helpful way to drive this point home is to think of every minute of the day as a decision in itself. You're either making an explicit decision to move forward or you're making an implicit decision to stick with the status quo, whether you're analyzing or not. If you find yourself or others on your team paralyzed and not making decisions quickly, reduce the scope until B and C are in tolerable ranges and then move forward on that mini decision. Whether you get from point A to point B through one big decision or a series of smaller ones, you still get to B. That being said, it's also better to get there through multiple smaller decisions, because this provides multiple points for new information and feedback to come into play. Momentum is everything in decision-making, and with this scope management technique, there are really no excuses to be making slow or nonexistent decisions.

Generate Alternatives
Another big area of decision failure is not generating enough alternatives. Some people are used to developing the first gut feeling they get and closing their mind. This approach is lazy and very often results in missing alternatives that could be much better. To unseasoned decision makers, this sounds trivial. To those that are good at making decisions, they know that generating a range of strong possible alternatives is central to innovation and groundbreaking solutions. The effort to generate alternatives is an activity that actually stimulates better decisions. I personally recommend always having at least three great alternatives in any situation, before you choose one.

Summarizing
Questioning is recognized as one of the most powerful ways to proactively manage our thinking as well as the focus of others in

conversation. Equally as powerful is the concept of summarizing. After discussions on a topic, there tend to be many loose ends. A good decision maker steps up to summarize and distill these into actions. The combination of questions and summarizing, along with follow-up, are some of the most important tools of management.

Follow-Up

One of the biggest failures with regard to decision-making is a lack of sustained follow-up. We've all attended business meetings or election pitches where endless well-intentioned promises are made. These promises are easy to state, and can successfully convince others to buy in to great ideas at no cost. Talk is cheap, as they say. It really is! The cost, and hence the real value, comes with actual delivery. We're all human. Is this something you struggle with, just like everyone else on the planet? It's human nature. Like fear, you can't avoid it. Don't avoid it. Manage it.

You Need External Measurement

When it comes to something as personal and demanding as big decisions, we can't rely on our own biased views to be realistic. We need to enlist trusted friends to provide honest assessment on our progress. Targets must be personal. So should our line of sight. But progress—in terms of actions and how we handle reactions— is best measured ourselves and corroborated by those we trust. It's easy to cut ourselves slack when we shouldn't.

Seek Trusted External Perspectives

We are all in our comfort zones in the way we think. Without seeking trusted external insights, we'll repeat the same decisions without realizing it. The context and situation may change, but our overall approach remains the same. Seeking external advice does not imply we put aside our own convictions or core beliefs. Instead, it often reaffirms them. We should take trusted external insight respectfully and then choose whether or not to incorporate it.

The importance of sourcing external perspectives when you make a decision isn't just to improve the decision. It's central to even making the right decision. Our mindset deeply and naturally reflects years of entrenched biases that we have found to be helpful. We can never truly think like anyone other than ourselves for this reason. The takeaway realization here is that you have to constantly talk with the audience you are trying to communicate with. The classic advice of putting a "zipper on it" and listening applies. You need to engage in active listening to gain true understanding. Active listening means asking questions, both open-ended and close-ended.

Are You Using Your Superconscious Mind?

Even if you are not trained in psychology, you understand the notions of the conscious and subconscious minds. The conscious mind characterizes the state when we're aware of ourselves and our own role in our environment. We're self-aware. It's where rational thinking occurs. In contrast, the subconscious mind is a state where we aren't logically aware of the decisions going on; we're driven by our emotions. We instinctively react to our environment in the way we've been conditioned to react through our physiology and/or societal experiences.

Our emotions can reflect instincts or learned behavior. Regardless, the subconscious is the core driver of human behavior. It can be supplemented by rational conscious thought, but even then, the conscious just brings us back to the emotions we want to experience and the ones we want to avoid. Life is emotions. Love, anger, fear, revenge, altruism—all these emotions are the only way we truly experience life. All rational thoughts eventually matter because they result in desirable emotional states.

Based on my experience, I feel the real opportunity exists in our superconscious. To me, the superconscious mind is in play when we proactively control the direction of our conscious mind. We're not just aware. We're using the full arsenal of tools, such as questions, neuro associative conditioning, visualization, and emotional immersion, in order to fully control our state.

We're all familiar with meditation; some of us even practice it. Meditation has been around since ancient times and is an incredible way to break away from external distractions. Meditation has mental and physical components and provides a way to remove external distractions by clearing the mind. It can give your mind and body a rejuvenating rest, and in today's hectic world the importance of this can't be understated.

The superconscious is similar to meditation in the sense that we clear the mind of distractions, but instead of clearing the mind we immerse it in a targeted focus. This targeted focus is emotional, visual, and logical. Think of a high you had in life—winning an award on stage, seeing your name in print, performing a song, or scoring a winning goal. All of us have experiences like this, even if from our childhood. You've hit your superconscious when all these factors are ticking in alignment. In this state you're in peak performance mode. It's the mental state that Usain Bolt is in when he's ready to run. Total control. Total focus. Results.

It's easy to talk about your superconscious, but in practice many of us are really bad at it. We're so used to jumping around sporadically in our thoughts. Society reinforces this. Superconsciousness requires sustained emotional and mental focus and energy. You need to be feeling the high of a visualized amazing outcome, like winning a major award, and cranking out the thoughts and actions that make it happen. It's all practice. You should practice this relentlessly and you'll get good at it.

To see what I mean about how hard it is, try this exercise when you have your next morning shower. Don't let your mind jump from one random external thought to another. Try for just five continuous minutes to maintain an excited emotional level and targeted complementary thoughts about a single line of sight. It's really hard. Practice until you get to five minutes, then ten minutes and then find a fifteen-minute activity and do it again.

Interrupts versus Autopilot

Interrupting your daily autopilot is absolutely critical to break the cycle of external influences that bombard you every day. There's a time and place though, when autopilot is equally as critical—when you don't want any interruptions. That time is when you need peak performance. Think of an Olympic athlete ready to compete in an event. He or she maintains complete focus to achieve top performance. Interruptions are disastrous in this peak performance situation. Autopilot is absolutely desirable and required here.

This peak performance scenario is opposite to typical day-to-day situations. In the latter, we need to adapt and learn as we face a barrage of external distractions. We aren't set up for autopilot like we would be in an Olympic event. In daily life, autopilot is dangerous. We need interruptions more than ever. Tony Robbins drives home the importance of creating interruption behaviors—small things that make you stop and shake up your current autopilot—to redirect where you want to focus. Your interrupt can be a simple physical action, like snapping your fingers, saying a crazy word to yourself, and so on—anything to jolt you out of autopilot.

These little and powerful interruptions are very effective in our daily lives. Sometimes you benefit from breaking out of your routine. It's liberating to do something crazy, like stopping at a park on your way to work and taking five minutes of your time to just daydream. Just hearing this scenario probably makes you think I'm crazy. But is it? When you were little, you did this all the time. I've done it. It's not crazy at all. It's a small step toward reinforcing your control over your time and mind. Don't have time? Get up five minutes early. Seriously.

I cannot stress enough how important it is to actually physically interrupt your routines. Whether it is as simple as snapping your fingers and changing your thinking track, or pulling over to the side of the road to gaze at the clouds. Habits drive your current outcomes. If you want new outcomes, you need new habits. Unless you think deeply about it, it's hard to appreciate how extensively our routine habits already impact our lives. How do you have your coffee? When do you have your coffee? How would you feel when these routines get shaken up? Are they similar to small addictions? No matter how great your autopilot habits are, you always need to challenge everything you do at some point, through powerful interrupts.

Finding Your Line of Sight

Many of us get excited at the thought of living a mission with passion, but without clarity on what drives us, we're stuck! Most people dream big; that's the fun and easy part. Some people even take action but find the fulfilment elusive. The way around this is to do what you did as a child. Just try things that seem slightly interesting and keep on doing them. You will find some things you like and you can shortlist from there. Passions in life do not come to us by sitting at a desk sketching notes. Get out, live life, and enjoy it. Once you're doing this, you'll find the things you like the most. If you're a pessimist and think this won't help you, you're wrong. If you actually do this, you will be happier.

Everyone Has a Split Personality

It's easy to place people into simple buckets. Some people are great; others are disdainful. Good and bad. We do this because such categories make it easier to make decisions. But the truth is that all people have elements of both. Each one of us can be incredibly good and incredibly bad, depending on our conditions. We are human. As a result, we adapt to our environment and our behaviors change. It's true that we all have a dominant lean to one side or the other. Some people are predominantly nice and others are generally jerks. It's important to keep this in mind in a decision-making context, because it means that people are highly predictable. But people can also surprise us, so make sure to build in this variance when evaluating stakeholders to your decisions.

A Common Element of Motivation

It's usually risky to generalize but there are consistencies across *all* people. Maslow's hierarchy of needs is an excellent example of a common framework of that drives all people. One of the most important motivations of every person is to belong to a group—to be needed and wanted—while at the same time being viewed as special in that group. It's only natural that we place ourselves at the center of importance. Our reality is our perception, which revolves around us. Remember this reality when forming your own decisions and when assessing the motivations of others as they relate to your decisions.

Is Your Dream Really a Dream?

Many people talk about dreams. Do you have one? Some of us have romantic ideas that pop into our heads, which we confuse with dreams. A real dream is actually a powerful decision. Olympic athletes are a great example. Competing at the Olympic level requires a decision that is a dream. Athletes are motivated by burning passion every minute of every day. They have clear sights, targets, actions, and reactions in the face of intense pain.

Understanding an athlete's decision is helpful for us to judge whether we truly have dreams. Olympic athletes do not simply define their decisions and move on. They literally visualize themselves holding the medal on the podium. They feel the pulse of their heartbeat. They smell the sweat of other athletes around them. They actually feel the aches and pains in their muscles. Then they feel themselves getting there. They replay their technique in their heads over and over. They can feel their muscles burn even as they just envision their techniques. They also relentlessly go over their physical moves.

Not every decision we make needs to be a dream at this level. This example should make us think about our true conviction. The terms *dreams* and *goals* get thrown around a lot. Realistically speaking, most of us should have a single dream rooted in a central sight. This sight stays core in most of our other decisions—with sub-decisions having smaller targets as they get more granular.

The Olympian example is helpful here again. Notice that the athlete doesn't dream about being a gold medalist. They dream about getting a gold medal in a particular sport, like sprinting, volleyball, or equestrianism. This seems obvious and far-fetched in our example, but we think it's okay to set our sights on "becoming an entrepreneur." But if you haven't nailed down the areas you're passionate about, like technology, finances, food, and so forth, then your "dream" is really just a wish.

Manage Your State

Your current mental state reflects the many neurological processes occurring at a given time. External or internal stimuli can determine your mental state, and your current mental state will impact how you interpret costs and benefits. Your underlying, long-term beliefs still drive things, but your current state has a very large influence. That's why top performers learn to control their own mental state. Elite athletes focus only on the task at hand, ignoring countless distractions. The same goes for musicians in performances. They aren't unaware of external influences, but they are so clearly driven by their internal thinking that they place the external elements into a supporting role, without missing a beat. Our current state is very powerful relative to longer-term beliefs because it is most synched with current raw emotions. That being said, long-term memories can be very powerful if they were filed away with an extreme emotion, such as trauma or exhilaration. You need to link pain and pleasure accordingly to achieve your goals. The way to do this is NAC (Neuro Associative Conditioning).

Neuro Associative Conditioning

CE literally defines what decisions are, both as a formal mathematical optimization of a utility function against a psychological cost/benefit trade-off curve, and with the practical formula of Decision = Sight + Targets + Action + Reaction. But to get results, we need tools and regimens that turn the ideas into reality in our behaviors. There's no need to completely reinvent the wheel here. A stellar model for personal change, which comes down to an applied decision process, is that of NAC, invented by Tony Robbins. NAC is grounded in the psychology of Neuro Linguistic Programming.

I don't believe you can successfully master decision-making without using NAC. I consider it a core tool in the CE decision toolkit. If you read Robbins' books years ago and have them tucked away on your shelf as you try to keep up with the newer gurus, pick them back up and read them again. If you don't have them, order them now. It is life-changing stuff, for business people, athletes, world leaders, and ... housewives building a side business and frustrated cubicle jocks. Basically, anyone!

Robbins demonstrates that we all own our own destiny through our beliefs. Our beliefs define our B and C perceptions. Each of us alone has the power to change how we see the world. You will be tested. But with the proper B and C perceptions in place, which essentially define your sight, you'll stick to it through targets, actions and reactions. This is a sobering reality for some—that happiness is truly in their control. Some people may be in rough situations, so it might take time, but eventually we will control our destiny through our decisions.

So how do you use NAC in this context? NAC is a step-by-step process which actually conditions your central nervous system. Following the six-step process for each decision will result in you associating massive pleasure to the benefits you want and massive visceral pain to the things you want to avoid or overcome. These associations aren't just mental ideas; they are actually physiological changes to your mind and body chemistry.

Step 1: **Decide What You Want and What Is Preventing You from That Outcome.**

Step 2: **Get Leverage.** Use pain and pleasure (cost and benefit) to associate massive pain to the status quo and massive pleasure to the desired state.

Step 3: **Interrupt Limiting Patterns.** Create shocking behaviors that are silly enough to jolt you out of your normal patterns.

Step 4: **Create an Empowering Alternative.** If you don't fill the void with a better option to become the new habit, you're likely to revert back.

Step 5: **Condition It.** Repeat the new behavior until it's an ingrained habit.

Step 6: **Test It.** You've got to monitor results to make sure your change sticks.

CE parallels NAC very closely. In Step 2, pain and pleasure parallel to cost and benefit. Steps 3 and 4 align with the personal total cost threshold in CE.

How Do You Know You're in the Right State of Mind?
Sometimes we have a great plan and are confident that we've got it figured out. We're confident from our *rational* side. We may feel an overwhelming energy, which is like rocket fuel every day. Our emotional side is driving us. Your right state of mind for success

has to be a natural high that combines these two things. If you're only leveraging one side or the other, you're not going to have the necessary staying power to see things through. When you have both elements ticking, you literally know it. You have that natural passion and natural high that gets you up early and into thought and action.

Values, Beliefs, Rules, and References
Tony Robbins also laid out very clearly the importance of values, beliefs, rules, and references. Values are the principles we believe in that sit at the core of our sights and everything else we do. You should definitely take the time to rank the values you want to live by and the ones you want to avoid. Beliefs are your perceptions of what's true and what isn't. They reflect your experiences and your attitude and frame everything you experience. The way you act is determined by your personal rules. These are the way you see causality in the world—what has to happen given that something else happened. References are the experiences we have logged in our mind that have built up our beliefs.

All these are important parts of the decision master system laid out by Robbins. It's worth the time to understand the nuances. However, in our context, CE translates all these components into an overall perception of personal cost and personal benefit in the short, intermediate, and long term. Everything boils down to this causal coupling, which makes it easy to remember and apply.

Risk Aversion
BE has demonstrated through extensive research that people are in general motivated twice as much by loss as they are by gain. That's how powerful risk aversion is and why the status quo is so hard to undo. If you're trying to understand why you or someone else isn't taking action, identify where the perceived risk lies. If you want to change the behavior, you must tackle this. Remember: "carrots motivate dreams and sticks motivate action."

Cost Aversion

A massive distinction to make with respect to CE is the concept of cost aversion versus risk aversion. Risk aversion, a concept well established in economics and psychology, is the desire to avoid *potential* costs. CE introduces cost aversion, because most decisions in life aren't just about potential costs—they usually entail actual costs that one must commit to bear upfront. For example, losing weight requires the cost of putting away the bag of chips and hitting the gym. If you add the concept of cost aversion to your thinking, in addition to risk aversion, it will put you miles ahead of others in understanding decision-making.

The Endowment Effect

The endowment effect is a very important behavior to understand in decision-making. It captures the reality that people don't want to give up what they have. This sounds obvious and is in line with the fact people avoid risk and cost more than they pursue benefits. But it goes deeper than that. If someone is given something for free and consider it their own, they won't want to part with it, even though they paid nothing for it. So be careful what you cling on to, and always know why.

Mental Accounting

Nobel economist Richard Thaler put forward an important theory called mental accounting. To simplify, this implies that decision makers simplify their choice set to overcome limited cognitive abilities. Not surprisingly such simplifications can reduce decision optimality, so one has to be careful. You'll probably find yourself doing some mental accounting, so I just want to make sure you knew where the theory came from.

Procrastination

Where to start on this one? Am I right in guessing that this one hits a personal sore spot with you? Is it the one that frustrates you?

I don't know anyone who doesn't struggle with procrastination. It's the deadliest of all barriers, because most of us are very comfortable with the status quo, and so alternatives indicating any kind of change represent higher costs. Even if the eventual benefits are higher, the cost to get there can be tough.

Procrastination arises when we logically feel we should be moving forward, but due to fear of change, we stay still and indecisive. You've probably heard the expression that the most dangerous word in the English language is "tomorrow." From a decision-making perspective, it is. It means we aren't feeling the urgency for change. The pain of the status quo hasn't hit our threshold yet. Procrastination is all about our motivation, and nothing to do with the actual situation. When we are procrastinating, we don't feel enough pain in the current situation and we feel that the pain of change outweighs the benefit, at least in the short term.

Get Physical

With so much focus on psychology and the importance of our mind, it is very easy to forget the absolutely vital role that physical experience plays. We live in our mind in many ways, but millions of years of evolution have allowed us to have a visceral connection to physical stimuli. This simply means that your physical stimuli matters. If you love the sun, go into the sun when you make big decisions. If you have childhood memories of a running stream, envision one and then go find one. This sounds like small stuff, but don't overlook it. Don't underestimate people who incorporate physical routines into their inspiration. Incorporate them yourself as well.

Get Visual—Literally

I'm a big believer in keeping a powerful reminder photo on your desk or a quote on the wall. You need to keep a visual front-and-center at all times. CE suggests we also add another key visual prompt— of the state you want to stay away from. The pain of the CODN (cost of doing nothing) has to be viscerally in your mind and soul at all times until it is gone. If possible, incorporate a time-based component, which can help with actionability.

Inspiration

I've said it before, but the most important factor in achieving your personal performance goals is to have an extremely emotional vision—complete clarity on where you "set your sights." The elements of the STAR decision-making framework in CE are prioritized in decreasing order. S is the most vital, followed by T, and so on. What this means is that with clear sight, the other elements follow. The clearer your line of sight, the greater the chance for the following phases of T, A, and R to progress.

Do You Really Know Your Own Values?

People do not take the time to write down their personal values, to identify what they see as positive/good and what they see as negative/most avoidable. Obviously the former makes up part of B and the latter part of C. Some C cannot to be avoided, and is required to achieve B. But there are certainly C factors that a decision maker sees as unprincipled, which should be avoided at all costs.

STAR: THE LINK BETWEEN SIGHT, TARGETS, ACTIONS, AND REACTIONS

I find that people often get confused between sight, targets, actions, and reactions. Many of us aren't used to defining decisions this thoroughly, so it's understandable. Your sight is a big-picture end state, a theme that runs through everything in your desired life at its core. For example, you may want financial independence by age fifty, to be an astronaut, to build a recognized charity, and so forth. These answer the question "what are the top three things you'd like to achieve with your life more than anything else?" There isn't just one. For many, it's common to have a sight for their family life, a sight for their career, and a sight for some kind of personal development goal. Sight isn't directly measured. It's measured through accomplishment of associated targets. Your sight is similar to your "why," a concept conveyed by Simon Sinek in his book by the same name.

Targets are specific outcomes at a certain point in time; for example, building a car dealership to $25 million in revenue within two years at 5 percent margin.

Actions are the actual activities required to hit the targets. With the car dealership target example, a set of actions may be to (1) open the store by February 2021 with an inventory of 100 cars, and (2) have four power sellers in place by June 2021.

Sight

Tired of Pep Talks?

If there's one thing I'd like to achieve more than anything else with this book, it's to make Causal Economics (CE) something that helps you every single day. My worst nightmare is something that happens so often with books. We read them, acknowledge solid ideas, get excited about them … and then … go back to our daily routine as if nothing has changed. So many distractions and people take up our time that this is normal. Add to the fact that most of us are pretty comfortable and do not feel an urgent, painful need to change.

A part of my personal sight is to make sure that I'm not just another motivational pep-talker that sells short-term passion boosts. There is plenty of that out there. I spent ten years trying to figure out a better approach to economics and decision-making because I wanted to come up with a new way that actually worked. I was tired of seeing short-term thinking, hand-out lobby politics and wasteful BS business meetings. If you're doing something you like, regardless of how much attention you get, you'll be able to look back and feel you placed your time where it was best invested.

Sight is definitely the hardest part of making powerful decisions. We've all heard stories of super passionate people who knew what they wanted so bad that the specific targets, actions, and reactions in the face of massive uncertainty all fell into place. There's a lot of truth to this. Without sight, the rest doesn't matter. Don't spend time on the rest. We all have one life to live. You've got to picture yourself in ten, twenty, thirty years and ask, *what did I do and why?* It has to be defined from within, not by external milestones like assets or flashy cars. Don't get me wrong. If financial freedom is part of your sight, it's great to have material things and to enjoy life.

What If You're Not Bill Gates?

Do I honestly think that everyone can be, or should be, living their life with a Bill Gates level of sight? No. For some people, it fits. For others, their sight is about incredible parenting, personal hobbies, charity, or whatever. What drives each of us will be personalized, but if there's one striking feature of personally defined successful people versus those who are unhappy, it's whether their perspective is inward to outward or vice versa. Don't let other people mess with your head on what you want to accomplish. Listen to advice and compare it to what's important to you.

Inside or Out?

Sight is not fluffy. We can see it in people we admire. Well-defined sight is so razor sharp that we can *feel* it in people and, inspired by their energy, may even consider jumping on board with them. We can tell the difference between the talkers and the doers—those who think in line with CE, backing up talk with action and bold reaction.

Interestingly enough, there's something at the root of the mindset of these people with sight. You can actually observe someone for five minutes and determine whether they're following a sight or drifting. Sounds like a stretch? Not one bit. So what is this powerful mind state? The formal psychological name is an "internal locus of control." An internal locus of control means that a person's mind is directed by internal thoughts first and foremost, as opposed to external reactions. The latter represents an "external locus of control." I challenge you to find examples of people who are highly successful with an external locus of control. Wait, I take that back. That's a distraction. Focus on yourself, not others!

Makes sense when you think about it, doesn't it? At this point you might be thinking these are great things if you already have them, but how do you get into this way of thinking with a passionate line of sight and an associated internal locus of control? That's a critical question. So many smart and energetic people want to improve their life but feel lost in terms of where to focus. They're searching for a reason, cause, and passion. I'd say the vast majority of readers and my students are actually at this point. This is where it's most fun to work with and help people, by the way.

Feel Good Right Now
When you listen to Tony Robbins, one thing that's loud and clear is that you can control your state on the turn of a dime. Each of us controls our state 100 percent, no matter what the outside world presents us. It does not mean it's easy. We can interrupt our current situation with an "out there" thought and action, while changing our state at the same time. We really can feel great all the time. So why don't you do it?

Motivation
One of the most prevalent questions is "how do I get motivated?" This parallels the question "what gets us to decide to actually change?" Without action, we have fiction. With sustained action, we actually have a decision. The key is the CODN/BODS ratio. When the perceived cost of the status quo is so painful that it's worse than taking action, we're motivated to change. Please don't think that motivation is a happy envisioning of a future outcome. That's fiction.

Clarity Is One Thing…. But How Do You Get Hungry?
We've spent some time looking at how you get yourself focused on a clear sight, which is a critical starting point. But "conceptual

sight" is the kind of thing we can dream about and view on paper. To make it real, we need to add intense emotions. This is a huge challenge many face. We lead very comfortable lives with high B/C attached to our daily status quo. If you think you want much more, you won't go anywhere unless you attach major emotional pain to the status quo and massive emotional benefit to alternative scenarios. You can't "reason" about emotions. By definition you have to feel them—which means experiencing pain and pleasure through visualization and actual action. You have to get used to envisioning yourself literally in desired states and enjoying them. Even more importantly, you have to get specific and emotional about pain in your current scenario. Nothing else drives change. You have to hit your pain threshold. If you're comfortable in life at present, picture yourself ten years from now and how you want to answer to your future yourself.

This does not imply you have to be angry about everything in life. You can be extremely happy with your family life and extremely frustrated about how your side business is going. Pain should be very specific and visceral. I'm not trying to bum you out. You may be apprehensive that negative energy is not motivating. That's BS. Motivation only comes from a combination of a positive sight for where you want to be and a negative sight of certain conditions in your status quo. A person who has this balance comes across as positive and determined on an urgent mission. Dissatisfaction with the status quo ends up being a positive driver as the person is confident he/she can make the necessary changes, no matter what.

Targets

Why is the term "target" used in the STAR framework instead of "goals"? It's simply based on the imagery invoked by a target. You can almost see the bull's-eye, when you say the word. It begs you to take a shot. The word "goal" has often been attached to poorly defined "decisions," like old resolutions. I'm certain you have heard about SMART goals: Specific, Measurable, Action-oriented, Realistic, and Time-Based. That's a great definition. In CE, targets should be specific, measurable, realistic, and time based. "Action-oriented" is so important that action is its own category in the STAR framework!

Actions

We've covered the importance of action extensively and that it's built directly into the core definition of a decision, as a pretty unique element of CE. Decisions get momentum from the action and reaction stages. Action sounds pretty straightforward, right? In many ways it is, but let's dig a little deeper, because action not done right can create way more pain than necessary and it doesn't guarantee success on its own.

Action with no direction through sight and targets burns a ton of energy. We're all human and this will eventually tire anyone out. Most of us have heard the expression "Lack of a plan is a plan to go nowhere." It's absolutely true. But there's a time and place for action without a plan. When you have formed a sight, there is no excuse for a lack of targets and action. However, if you haven't yet nailed your sight, it is really important to take action without clear direction, or you won't uncover any inspiration.

Getting your action plan right is important. We've all either experienced or observed analysis paralysis. It's natural. Analysis keeps us from thinking about outcomes and avoiding the cost of the execution. Are you the one who gets endlessly preoccupied in writing down your action plan? Or do you avoid writing it down? Either extreme isn't ideal. It's very important to document quick and simple action plans in a few bullets. They should fit on your one-page personal plan.

Testing

A formal element of CE theory is the concept of testing. Where mainstream economic theory is centered around equilibrium, CE is a disequilibrium theory, with a unique twist. Equilibrium suggests that economies are systems that converge once available information is incorporated. Information and information asymmetry are the reasons equilibrium can be breached. In CE, information isn't at the root of decisions; motivations and incentives are. As a result, economic activity moves in trends, not equilibrium. Equilibrium is impossible in CE.

The concept of testing within CE asserts that even if an economy were to come close to an equilibrium, someone would test—take an action—to try new opportunities for gain. They aren't uncovering hidden information; they're creating new opportunities through innovation.

What does testing mean to you? It's a key way of thinking to help you focus on action. Testing is momentum, taking action. You can only learn more and create more, never less, by testing yourself in a new direction. My advice is to test your assumptions and those around you as you take action!

Reactions

The idea of "reaction" as a distinct element beyond action derives from the concept of causal coupling. Reactions are actions in the face of barriers and challenges. We take action first and then give a reaction, based on how we deal with the resistance from the initial action. The distinction reflects the reality that upfront costs are required through action and reaction—before there is any possibility of future benefit.

When it comes to action planning, a great approach is to identify action items and anticipated reactions. Therefore, you'll build your plan in a premeditated manner, thinking how you'll act when a specific challenge arises. This helps you make your decision as much as possible before the intense emotion of the moment of the decision kicks in. Mapping out actions and reactions is an important nuance. Doing this places maximum focus on "doing" and explicitly addresses how we plan to tackle inevitable challenges. Without this technique, it's easy to put down noncommittal decisions and revise them when we miss.

GETTING BETTER AT DECISIONS

Never Forget Robinson Crusoe

When you're evaluating situations, it's a great idea to go back and imagine the basics in a "Robinson Crusoe" economy. In such a situation, nothing is accomplished unless someone does it. In such a small society, it's very obvious who is honestly contributing and who is not. "Working the system" will stand out and not be tolerated. Where someone can't contribute, other citizens can provide help.

In large societies like ours, where relationships are stretched and far removed, free riders will blend in more easily. There are so many layers that citizens cannot see what's actually going on in. While debating others, keep it simple: who is contributing and who is trying to free ride. Free riders will create all kinds of complexity to hide their actions in plain view. If you follow the idea of causal coupling, you will quickly be able to see who is contributing and benefiting and who is benefiting without contributing. The more society achieves the former, the more fair and sustainable it will be, because those building it can see fruits of their labor and those not so inclined can see what's required to get ahead.

Practice: Powerful and Dangerous

Effective decision-making is a combination of smarts and practice. If you're a seasoned decision maker who makes many good decisions, we're not suggesting you go through a bunch of processes to follow a model. People in such situations usually just give quick mental check marks to each of the components of a decision—sight, targets, actions, and reactions—to keep a handle on where they're at. Seasoned experts also quickly think about each stakeholder from the stakeholder perspective and mentally verify that their decisions achieve causal coupling, so they're fair and sustainable. Causal Economics (CE) becomes a part of their mindset and way of thinking, just like they've had a more traditional view of economics and psychology in the back of their minds when gauging people and policies.

If you're not currently at that level, you can benefit from a more "tool and template"-driven approach. We'll share a few such methods later in this book. At this point, it's vital to emphasize that *practice is key*. Decisions are often required in time-sensitive, emotionally charged situations, which requires you to be able to stay focused and make the best decision, often resisting emotional pressure from external sources that are not in your favor.

Practice is a double-edged sword; it's the key ingredient to mastery. The practiced expert has tested every nuance and optimized its reaction. Exceptional achievers relentlessly practice. Don't take practice for granted. On the flip side, it's important to use practice appropriately. Practice gets you into a routine, which makes it more challenging to introduce new perspectives. Your thinking can become automated and instinctual. As you become more practiced, make sure you put effort into opening your perspectives too, so you don't become an expert in the irrelevant. This happens very often, especially in business and technology.

We all know the famous saying about an "apple a day..." I suggest you also make three explicit and important decisions a day. Remember the phrase "three decisions a day!" This means writing them down—in bullets—to highlight what sight is driving them, what specific targets you will pursue, what actions you will take, and what reactions you will take when you hit resistance. Keep a log of them handy at all times—in your pocket or on your phone. At the end of each week, review them and see how you're doing. Identify the gaps and close them. Don't erase your notes on the gaps. That will mentally put you back to square one, by ignoring progress and not taking your actions seriously. You will be wrong often, so what? Don't let gaps or slow progress set you back. Success comes when you overcome.

How Should You Measure Your Success?

Making decisions is great, but not for their own sake. We're after *results*, which is why we can't be decisive if we don't have clarity around our sight and targets. Otherwise we're simply taking action aimlessly—there's nothing to measure against, so how can you be considered successful by your own lack of standards?

Take time on sight and targets. There's no doubt that some people will accuse you of actually being indecisive when you do this (ironic, isn't it?). Ignore them. When it comes to action and reaction, you'll be on fire, while they stand there scratching their heads.

It's simple. Measure you decision-making against each of your planned STAR elements. What percentage are you tracking to? To what percentage is each causally coupled across stakeholders—to ensure buy-in and sustainability? Then measure achievement (in percentage) against results. Keep measuring each decision like this and you'll get better at it.

Have Fun

Many readers are serious individuals who want to accomplish great things. As a result, we focus a lot on serious discussions. Let's pause for a moment. We have one life to live. We're blessed with this unique opportunity. So make your mark in your own way. All of us want to belong and be important. No matter how individualistic we are, this *want* is still at the core of the human psyche. We want to be seen as great individuals and part of a community. This motivates us to work very hard to achieve great things. But it's also important to not forget to have fun every day. If you're always serious, you won't appreciate the true beauty of life. This is deeper than enjoying what you do. Many of us enjoy what we do and still bust our butts so much we don't even have time to breathe. Making time for fun allows us to strike a mental and physiological balance, which makes us overall happier. Live life; achieve your wildest dreams and have a whole lot of fun while doing it!

The Super Big Picture

I'm sure we've heard this before. When someone's at the end of their journey on Earth, they don't wish they'd worked more hours, and so on. People who feel fulfilled place priority on relationships with those they love and their own personal development. If one has lived their life being invested in those they love and in themselves, being the best person they could, they've done the best they can on this planet. If you make a breakthrough, you can leave a legacy. There's no harm in that too, as long as one doesn't sacrifice their actual life to create a "virtual one" after they're gone.

Bad Outcome, Bad Decision... Right?

Results are what matter, right? Be careful with this line of thinking. It's what most of us have at times, because sensationalism sells in the media and our social circles. "Big wins" must mean brilliant decision-making. Massive failures must mean disastrous decision-making. Or at least that's how the headlines read. That kind of "wow" storytelling is just human nature. But please realize it's rarely reality. You cannot link decisions directly to results on a one-to-one basis, because you cannot control the world. All you can do is make decisions, and make them in the right way. Never forget this when people try to tie your one-off results to your decision-making capabilities. However, some people use this legitimate disconnect as an excuse. It's not, because the relationship between decision-making abilities and results does hold true in the longer term.

Bad decision makers can hide to some degree in the short term, with individual decisions, by blaming others and their circumstances. They can also lay claim to amazing decisions that they didn't really deliver—also in the short term. In the long term, our efforts in any discipline in life—decision-making included—are tied to the results. This is the ultimate example of causal coupling. In a free society, overall benefits generally reflect our overall costs over time, as we all zig and zag, learning from each decision and getting more refined each time.

Shrink or Expand the Scope Until You Can Act

Always make multitiered decisions. Every big decision has associated component decisions, and every small decision is part of a bigger decision. Too often, this simple reality is overlooked. We find ourselves stewing over stressful decisions, indecisive and inactive. Or we find ourselves taking steps forward but feel we don't know how they fit into the bigger picture, so we think we might be off track.

When you find yourself in decision inertia, it could be because the decisions are rolling up into one big decision. Of course, this may make us freeze as we seek more information and stare at huge risks. Anyone can make decisions. *Anyone!* As long as the decision is within the comfort zone. It's true that we have to push out of our comfort zones to achieve new things, but this should be incremental, as we build experience and clarity. For some, getting a bag of chips from the cupboard is a comfortable decision; for others, it is launching a new company. Perspective and experience are central. This means that you may need to shrink your scope of decisions down to a size you can reasonably handle at the current point in time or it may paralyze you. It does not mean that you lose sight of the big decision you're working on. Keep it in your mind, but create smaller, more manageable decisions to get you there.

On the flip side, if you find yourself being decisive and taking great action, but feeling that you're just puttering along without clarity or meaning, you may also have to increase your scope of decision-making. What's likely missing is clarity around your sight and targets. With those in place, every decision is cut and dry. This is the time to keep moving with your smaller decisions and setting aside time to concurrently build your big-picture decisions, which will provide you with the missing sense of clear purpose.

Decision-making is always multitiered because individuals are multitiered. Long- and short-term motivations are at the heart of everything we do.

Don't worry, at least you're not this guy.
In 2019, a Darwin Award was bestowed upon an experienced U.S. pilot/ instructor who decided to calmly keep flying without thinking there was a problem when his cockpit filled with liquid fuel. Confidence is great, but this no doubt crossed the line. He died. I'll bet you haven't made a decision that bad—since you're still here. So don't be too hard on yourself.

How Long Should a Decision Take?
Most people think of decisions as a choice made from which they move on to the next thing. This is far from the truth. You're probably not surprised at this thinking, given today's short-term focused world and given that our existing decision models are based on

single-period thinking. Real-life decisions span multiple periods of consideration as to when they're being made and when they're being implemented. This is the core divergent thinking of CE. A decision takes as long as you define it to. You select the relevant time horizon for a particular decision. Some decisions will apply to our entire life, such a decision about religious faith. Some will be instantaneous and simple. CE allows all these time horizons to be modelled, where alternative theories don't. Think from a CE perspective and you'll be on track to your sights and targets that exceed a single period.

But Decisions Are Hard, Aren't They?

In a world of limited time and resources, change takes effort against vested interests. The most important decisions in life are hard because they require very deliberate upfront cost (time, effort, money) in anticipation of future, less certain, benefits. This is the central thread of CE—causal coupling—which is missing from other decision models. Causal coupling is what makes decision theory fit into reality, taking it out of the lab and constrained mathematical models.

The great thing about decision-making is that it is undoubtedly a skill. That means we can become better, and exceptional, through practice. Later in this book, we'll share some great exercises to help you practice, whether you're an entry-level employee or a CEO.

One of the toughest parts of decision-making is arriving at an emotionally powerful sight. It is easy for idea-driven personalities to drift from concept to concept in a coffee shop. I've been there. A lot of us have been there. Lack of focus is the first tough part that can kill decisions. It sounds like a lack of discipline, but it actually isn't. The missing ingredient goes deeper.

It's the pain threshold for change. Tony Robbins conveys this masterfully through NAC concepts in his seminal work *Unlimited*

Power. When someone's life is pretty comfortable, it's high benefit and low cost fun to keep thinking and not worrying about the grind of implementation. New, even better, ideas are around the corner, giving hope and letting us off the hook for not "doing" the last one. Without emotional pain, there's no sight for change. You have to get really frustrated with the status quo or you won't drive change. That's reality.

Tough decisions often go with tough conditions, like financial hardships or other life challenges. Making tough decisions is definitely not easy, and for those in dire circumstances, such as poverty, the costs can be extremely high. A lot of our focus here is on aspirational decision-making, the type of improvement that fortunate individuals have the luxury to make. It's important to remember that without effective and empowered decision-making in extremely tough situations, other coping mechanisms including destructive addictive behavior can occur. We benefit from making the best possible decisions we can as we try to improve in life over time. My point here is that decision-making is serious business and individuals should aim to be better at it for their own gain and to help their fellow citizens.

Incredible Advice from Robert Treliving, Founder of Boston Pizza and TV Dragon

Jim Treliving has a very unique perspective. A business magnate, he started out as a Royal Canadian Mounted Police (RCMP) police officer in Canada. He's one of few people who really has seen it all—board rooms and back alleys! In his recent book titled *Decisions*, he shares what he considers the most important business lesson of all: to "do something—make a decision and go!" What a way to drive home our thinking in this book. He illustrates how training our psyche to decide and take action in the face of any circumstance propels us forward, versus the psyche that freezes in the face of actual or potential fear.

Treliving lays out five great principles which definitely align with our discussions:

1. **Get over Fear**—make decisions despite fear.
2. **Reward Loyalty**—you can't build unless you and your partners are mutually loyal.
3. **The Only Thing You Can Control Is Your Attitude**—Jim illustrates perfectly causal economic decision-making—avoiding a corrosive attitude of pain and pursuing a winning attitude of gain. He puts the B/C ratio wildly in his favor because that's what he can control.
4. **Remain Entrepreneurial**—this is self-explanatory; keep close to the decision, not bureaucracy.
5. **You Can't Repair Bad Word of Mouth**—your reputation is everything; don't risk it by getting ahead of yourself. A good reputation/brand means others see a high B/C associated with you. A bad reputation means a very low B/C association.

Treliving's principles align with and illustrate CE decision-making in action. He maximizes his own B/C and ensures that of his partners is also maximized. And instead of holding back and letting C take over, he keeps momentum to go after B and wins.

Can We Make Decisions Easier?

So how can we make decisions easier? Are we doomed to struggle with demons when making change? Not necessarily. Decisions are hardest when the B/C and level of C involved take us into new territory, with relatively high levels of C and low levels of B/C. This means that decisions are harder when they push against our beliefs. The latter drives our very perceptions of B and C. This comes down to the reality that if we take the time to get our beliefs where we truly want them, and build passion around them, it becomes easier to make decisions consistent with them.

It's All about Pain in the End

Get comfortable with pain. High performers are. They aren't scared of it; they overcome it. It's well-documented and proven in practice that pain motivates twice as much as pain. It makes sense in a dangerous world where one has to survive. Risk aversion can literally save our lives. That's why it's a natural state. We naturally and lazily pursue gains where there is little cost or risk involved, but we jump into action/effort to avoid risk and danger. There's only one time we will take massive action to obtain gain: it's when we feel intense pain in our current status quo. So once again, it is pain that truly motivates us. The gain we seek is just our sight to get away from the pain we feel today. If we don't feel massive pain in our current situation, we're comfortable and our psyche can't drive super hard for something new. This isn't a negative viewpoint. It's reality and you need to understand it to drive change.

Why are you really unhappy with your current sales numbers? Your job? Your relationships? If you can't place raw emotional pain with these, you honestly won't go after your benefit goals. In fact, we often define our massive gain targets as states that exactly get us out of our undesired scenario, and put them far away in our rearview mirror.

CE introduces a personal total cost threshold (PTCT) curve. This is the pain breaking point necessary for change. It can change over time, but is fixed for a current particular decision as it's built up on a lifetime of highly emotional experiences. It's also represented as the change ratio of the CODN/BODS (cost of doing nothing/benefit of doing something).

What this means for you as a decision maker is to evaluate, in every case, where your change ratio is and where that of others is. That's how you separate talk from action. You can get a sense of where your own is and where that of other decision makers is, by observing past decisions objectively. Don't just listen. Watch. Watch them on the golf course, like Jim Treliving does, to see what they're really like.

Isn't No Decision Better than a Bad Decision?
An excuse sometimes used to avoid tough decisions is that no decision is better than a poor decision. It's not true. "No decision" represents a lack of focus and action, which is not to be confused with actively choosing the status quo, which is *still* a decision. Since a lack of decision contains no momentum, one cannot move closer to sights and targets. That's why a lack of decisions is so dangerous.

What about taking actions that we later find out were not the best ones? As long as you defined your sight, set measurable targets toward it, took action, and reacted with conviction to obstacles, you made a good decision. If you didn't gain the results you wanted, then each of the STAR elements can be reviewed for optimization. The point here is that you can't predict and/or fully control the future. That's the cost of freedom itself. You can only map your own course and go for it. Unexpected results show us how to improve based on information we didn't have. I believe the inertia that comes with not making decisions creates a habit that is costlier than the poor decisions made.

The worst thing you can do in the long term is get in the habit of not making decisions and accepting the status quo. Because the status quo will continue to shift against the truant decision maker (you) as others continue making decisions to their advantage. Allowing the habit of avoiding decisions is a condition that only gets worse. In the short term, this behavior will probably not be noticeable, but it will always catch up in the long term—with bigger costs.

The Three Phases of Learning—Listen, Do, Teach
Many of us are used to the "listen" phase of learning. That's what occurs in formal schooling at all levels. Teachers/instructors bestow knowledge, ideally based on their own expertise. A quick digression is in order at the outset. Have you heard of the expression "those that can't do, teach"? A career in education/academia

does not usually tie to or allow for much applied real-world experience. The listening phase of learning is critical and saves years of trial and error if your teachers have actual practical experience. Be aware of whether they do and interpret accordingly, and supplement where needed.

The second phase of learning is "doing." This is instilled during apprenticeships and co-op programs and is incredibly important. But in life, no one has prearranged such programs for you, so you have to build them yourself. You don't need a formal program per se. You just have to think in terms of practicing—and do it. If you don't internalize this phase as a habit, you may end up like those highly educated people who don't get hands-on expertise in their fields but can still sound like experts and talk a great game. Without experience, no one truly understands the nuances of the things that really matter. Beware.

The third stage of learning is "teaching." Once you have traveled through the previous two stages, you can become an expert when you must distill your insights to others. This requires you to tighten up your thinking and cover gaps. True masters continually go through these three phases to hone their craft.

Another thing to be wary of is the "expert" that covers Phase one and jumps to Phase three. This is common in academia and consulting due to the career paths. It's important to learn from experts in formal academic environments (university/college), but never rely on them alone. Always ensure that you have hands-on experts to role model. This is the only way you'll get the "doing" insights in most cases.

Beware of Stretch Goals

There's perhaps nobody in business who hasn't heard of or been a part of "stretch goals." They're critical in decision-making but, when not done correctly, they can have drastically negative impacts. In fact, stretch goals are one of those things that we can get much better at through practice. Practical decision makers are able to set the goal just "stretchy enough." Those without enough practice generally fall into one of two categories. The unseasoned "go-getter" often has great sight, but sets unrealistic goals, which cascades into frustration and demotivation. The unseasoned "coaster" often sets goals that are too easy and doesn't push enough to drive real change and innovative results. There's no magic formula to getting this right. It takes observation and practice to find the rhythm that's right for you.

Don't Go around Telling Everyone Your Targets

Some common advice includes making your objectives public to help add pressure to keep you on track. This isn't generally helpful, so be wary. It makes sense to share your personal sights with people who appreciate it when someone's on a mission. Such people can provide supporting energy and insights. And you can do the same for them. Indulging in this kind of sharing with people who don't live with similar levels of passion is a waste of time and a potential "bring me down" invitation. Talk about the weather with such people!

Life and Death or Trivial?

We've been speaking in general to a large degree. So it's important to step back and appreciate the critical difference between decisions that are life and death and those that are more trivial on the other end of the spectrum. The B and C profiles of your current situation will make clear likely change if any. Comfort breeds very different decisions than desperation. Always understand where you and others stand on this spectrum before you try to predict outcomes.

Confidence and Humility

The answer to most things in life usually involves some sort of yin and yang—a balancing act or moderation. This isn't philosophical; I mean it practically. When it comes to decision-making, you need to operate from a place of confidence. If you let your confidence waver, your emotions can throw you off. We all have fears and they won't go away in tough situations. It shouldn't, as the emotion is present to protect us. But we have to keep confidence-sapping emotions from becoming prohibitive.

In addition to this confidence, humility is critical. Over-confidence easily becomes arrogance. It's very easy to fall into this trap when the going is good. When the going gets bad, this artificial, ego-driven arrogance collapses and old "heroes" become vulnerable. Whether in decision-making or leadership, this balanced combination of true confidence and genuine humility is required for success in the long term. All great leaders have this balance.

Great Advice from Robert Herjavec, Tech Leader and TV Dragon

Canadian tech business leader and TV celebrity Robert Herjavec provides one of the best real-world examples of causal coupling in action. In his book *The Will to Win*, he lays out that problems are problems first and opportunities later. This is a very pragmatic realization of causal coupling; effort must precede success—cost must always precede benefit. He also reminds us that relentless effort and optimism are key, but we must also focus on reality over platitudes.

In the same book, Herjavec points out that "nobody deserves anything." He points out that he and his family came to Canada with very little and he built success through his own effort. He put in massive C to obtain massive B. And it was worth it. Here are a few statements from this book that drive the point home so clearly, that B must follow C, that it must be causally coupled:

- "No one deserves anything except the right to prove ourselves."
- "No one owes any of us a thing: we each get from life what we make of it."

- "The only person responsible for your success or failure is the person you look at in the mirror every morning."

Herjavec's views reflect a powerful motivation to overcome bullies who tried to hold him back in his personal life as well as a unique opportunity to observe Eastern and Western Europeans' attitudes toward success. The ability to put in C to achieve B in the West, bullies aside, lit his fire. Look what happened.

Examples from Your Experience
We've looked at a number of real-life decisions, some of which are probably familiar to you. But there's no better way to apply and learn from CE than by applying it to some of the actual past decisions you've made. Take a moment to come up with one decision you look back on as a big failure and another you think of as a great success.

For each decision, create a column for cost and a column for benefit and add bullet points to reflect factors you saw as relevant at the time of the decision. Then leave some space and add factors you identified as C and B after the decision was made.

Be a Mini Historian
I'm not suggesting you pursue a degree in history or read books that cover the entire history of mankind. Unless that in itself is central to your sight, you're certainly not going to have time. But a high-level read of history is very important. No doubt you're awesome, but remember there is a long list of brilliant people before you. You and I are not the first people to face the type of problems we face today. Part of not reinventing the wheel on decision-making comes down to having historical awareness, which can bring to light costs and benefits that did not previously come to your mind.

Three Decisions a Day
At a bare minimum, I suggest all of you should practice making at least three significant decisions each day. This means having the

STAR elements defined and making an entry in your decision log. Practice makes … you know … perfect. Enough said on that one!

Kill the Clutter

We've hit extensively on the vital importance of focus—both on benefits to pursue and costs to avoid. The opposite of focus is clutter or noise. It closely competes with procrastination as the number one barrier to success for most people. It is usually with good intention that we gather all the information we can and try to process it with the importance we feel it deserves. After all, we don't want to miss a thing. And information is power, right? No. Information is power only if it gets you ahead. Most information is noise, which makes you freeze in inaction. Whenever information comes your way, you have to brutally triage it just like a hospital ER nurse. Anything else will take away from your priorities and distract you with a busyness that does not propel you toward your destination.

Read Like a Maniac

As much as we try to be masters of our own destiny, our environment will shape us—no matter how smart we are. You become what you're around, as the saying goes. Keep in mind that STAR isn't eliminating the importance of external insight. It's designed to help us control our perceptions and map out our journey within them. Very often, focused people have a high internal locus of control, so they may be guilty of not keeping their reading at the level it should be. We're each just one person in a world of many smart people. We can draw incredible insights from others out there who've had the kind of success we're seeking.

Don't reinvent the wheel; learn from them. Like everything else in life, committing to reading is itself a decision. You have to make it align to what you've set your sights on and set explicit targets. Successful people set aside a fixed amount of time every day for reading. I personally was behind on my reading and had to make this an important decision in my decision log. Now I'm fully on track.

Reverse Role Modelling

We've all heard a lot of talk on the importance of role modelling. It lets us observe successful people and emulate what they do, and is a powerful way to ensure we aren't reinventing the wheel. There's no question that I recommend role modelling. But it's also true that we learn the most from mistakes. We're all motivated twice as much by pain than by pleasure. Failures sting. So, there's a missing ground in the middle—a combination of the concept of role modeling and learning from our mistakes—which I call reverse role modelling. Reverse role modelling is observing and learning from the failures of others, specifically to ensure that you don't mimic those failures.

How Much Rest Are You Getting?

Nobody wants a nagging lecture on eating our vegetables or getting enough sleep. So you've probably rolled your eyes and closed your mind to this section, right? Hey, don't do anything for me. For your own good, you need to get enough rest in order to hit and sustain peak potential. If you're serious about peak performance and getting into a state of superconscious, then you need to pay attention to this section. Rest doesn't just mean sleep. Though you need enough sleep for sure. Don't skimp on it repeatedly or you'll hit lows, not highs. Rest also means giving your brain a break during the day. Take a quick ten-minute walk at lunch and even meditate when possible. If you don't give actual downtime to your brain, emotions, and body, you will burn out. That is physiology and biology. Sorry to break it to you, but you're arrogant if you don't take this point seriously.

How Competitive Should You Be?

There are people who are competitive in every single thing they do—even silly stuff (like getting into the elevator first!). This relentless pursuit of success should give you assured success, no? So how competitive should you be?

The answer is very competitive, but with a few vital nuances. You should be competitive with yourself first and foremost and only on things that align with your line of sight and targets. If you're competing in other areas, you're detracting from focus and wasting energy. It's therefore acceptable to compete with others, as long as it's moving you toward your own desired outcomes. This is important because competing with others who don't have focus will reinforce an external locus of control.

I Guarantee Your Decisions Turned Out Better Than This One.
In 2018, a religious missionary and explorer decided to make contact with the completely isolated Sentinelese tribe in India—to offer them eternal life. They killed him. Stay positive… have you really made a decision this bad? Obviously not if you're reading this.

Sight Lines Are Two-Sided
Vast attention is given to visualizing the desired end state you seek in goal setting. We're encouraged to see, taste, feel, hear, and smell our desired outcome, immersing ourselves in our end state. Yes, this is super important, but you simply cannot stop here. It's dangerous to stop here. This kind of positive thinking takes us on a high, as we experience B nonstop. And that's the issue. We need to feel just as viscerally about the state we want to avoid at all costs. We know pain motivates twice as much as pleasure, so we have to feel it intensely too. Real change begins when people feel pain beyond their own personal pain threshold, where they can no longer tolerate the cost of doing nothing. For example, a person who makes it out of poverty to become a sports celebrity has done everything humanly possible to escape his or her current situation. Such a person's desired end state is a passion they enjoy and a route away from intense pain.

If you only envision the upside of your line of sight, you're leaving out the most important part of motivation. It's less pleasant, as you now intensely feel B and C, but if you want to actually change instead of just feeling good dreaming about change, make sure you have this two-sided view of your sight lines.

Know Your Levers

So much of our attention has been on the internal mental elements of decision-making. And so it should be. We need to start with getting our own head straight. But as we've indicated from the outset, our view of decision-making has to include action and reaction. Adding this real-world element of execution means that we have to be aware of and actively manage resources to get things done. Money, time, and focus need to be lined up by ourselves and via others—especially when it comes to securing support from others required to scale our results.

We need to consider these in advance and in the present, because they are the reality of actually acting with decisions. The S and T phases are all about B—thinking about great things is easy and fun. The A and R phases are mostly about C—facing opposition and putting in efforts, which could be tough and not always fun.

How to Predict Anything

You can be a master in predicting the results of any initiative, if you simply look at whether it's based on the easy part—information—or whether it actually couples cost and benefit. When cost and benefit are coupled, benefit comes to those who contribute and costs only arise when benefits are delivered. This initiative is self-sustaining.

Most government programs fail because they do the easy things—relentlessly distributing information and rules. Politicians are rewarded for delivering great information (ideological speeches). They're not rewarded or held accountable for *actual results*. Not surprisingly, most government agenda is information sharing and administration.

Power and Negotiation

We haven't discussed the impact of power and importance of negotiation in the context of CE. Power and its projection, through negotiation, impact the C and B calculations of those involved in decision-making. When making decisions, be aware of power and the effect negotiation has, because people may adhere to C and B judgments, which change with shifts in the power structure. If you're not aware of how such dynamics play out, you may get multiple surprises as the landscape shifts and people revise their decisions as their power shifts.

Are You Childish Enough?

So what's the way forward? How does one leap from a comfortable, distraction-filled life to an all-consuming mission? I won't pretend that it's easy, but I will share how it's done by successful people. To make it happen, you have to add another element to the internal locus of control. You have to try new things and reflect on them. Too many people complain that they haven't found their passion; they expect passion to fall out of the sky. We were all children once and for many of us that was the last time we excitedly tried out everything new we could. We wanted to try everything. And we did. We did more of what we enjoyed and less of other things. We lived each day with passion and energy.

Thinking how we were as children is one of the biggest insights we can take away from reading this. Thinking about childhood is the furthest possible thing from being childish! My wife will personally testify that I subscribe to this philosophy personally. Like a lot of guys, I never really grew up.

So what changed for most of us? The outside world started to define us more and more. The bombardment of "no" and "you can't do that" started to define our view. If you're wandering about without passion, get out and try things that you used to enjoy as a kid as well as totally new things. Your personality reflects your core passions, even if you've suppressed them. As you try things, reflect on them honestly and keep your One Pager up-to-date; constantly prioritize more and more and narrow in on what will be your sight.

Does Scarcity Really Matter?
The traditional definition of economics is how people choose allocations of goods and services in the face of scarcity, generally reflected through pricing and budget constraints. The ultimate decisions around survival definitely center around scarcity. It does fundamentally matter, but not in the way economics invokes it. People don't always take scarcity as given and make price/quantity trade-offs. Some people will adjust their consumption in response to physical scarcity, but others will take the situation as inspiration to invest more for the future to create abundance—less future scarcity. How we interpret scarcity itself impacts how we behave. This has been largely omitted from economic modelling since the time of Adam Smith.

The one constant constraint we all face, whether a janitor or a CEO, is time. But even that is managed differently by different individuals. Some people sell their time by the hour in business, with no leverage—they work a job. Some build an organization with employees to scale their own time, but maintaining ownership. In the end, money is just "packaged" time. Obtaining money gets you access to the time of others, so you can hire them to work on the less engaging things in life, and devote your own personal time to living a great life.

When to Keep Your Mouth Shut
In today's hyper-connected world, many people spill their entire private life onto their social media profiles. I believe there's an entire generation or two that don't even understand the concept of keeping some things private. The world is full of good and bad. If you expose everything about yourself, you put yourself at risk

in the long term. You telegraph strengths and weaknesses that others can exploit. Choosing to be private in many areas of your life is not being dishonest. Your business is your business. Anyone who thinks your credibility depends on you spilling your inner thoughts on everything is arrogant and is too externally focused. Ignore them. Manage your reputation and your brand smartly. Today, information can be spun by others seeking to gain at your expense. Information and media have truly become weaponized, so keep this in mind when making your decisions.

Watch Others in Action

As you develop your own mastery of decisions, you'll get lots of practice by explicitly observing the decision processes of very successful and less successful people. It can be fun to see a situation facing a famous person and play along with a little "what would I do?" You can often analyze areas where decisions are getting their power or weakness—sight, targets, action, reaction. Even though this is a great way to exercise decision-making, it's no substitute for making many decisions and mapping them out in disciplined fashion.

If It's Not Written Down, It's BS

The written language is how we turn wandering thoughts into precise statements. When you're defining your decisions and tracking them, you need these things written down and visible throughout your day. The world is full of distractions and your brain responds to triggers. So why don't you drive your own triggers instead?

Taking notes also sends a message to others. Imagine you're a senior executive at your company. Not taking down a single note to confirm what you've understood can be insulting to others. It sends a message that you don't care and are not seriously considering what they're saying—the opposite of active listening. It undermines trust no matter what level of power the players are at.

You Can Entirely Predict Who Will Be Reliable in Decision-Making

There's a virtually foolproof way to determine who will actually follow through on your decisions as expected and who will make and follow through on their own decisions. The three major indicators are the *verbal commitment* to a decision, the *written commitment* to a decision, and the *proactive follow-up* associated with a decision. If someone won't state back their decision, they are not buying it. If they don't write it down, they don't take it seriously. If they do not proactively drive forward the decision and demonstrate it publicly, they aren't truly passionate about it either. These three indicators are very specific manifestations of being bold in words and then following through on words consistently.

The Biggest Barrier to Effective Decision-Making

I'm convinced that the number one barrier to great decision-making is the *attitude* of the decision maker. I discovered this by finding parallels to my early experience as a stock trader. Making money in trading in the long term always comes down to boring management of the odds. It was never the result of the huge windfalls we hear about in lore.

Professional traders use historical probability distributions so they know what their likely odds are. They hold to exit points in their trades that produce a win/loss ratio of something like 3 to 1. This implies that they expect to be wrong on as many as three out of four trades. As long as each of the losses are at most 1/3 of the expected gain on the winning trade, they can still break even. The bottom line is that with the right approach, you can be guaranteed to make consistent profits over time in the markets. You can also easily tell who'll make money and who'll lose it by observing their behaviors. If this is the calculated approach of winners, what's the alternative followed by money-losing traders? Losers expect to win all their trades. They're more focused on being right than they are about the results of making money.

It's the same thing with decision-making in general. You can tell horrible decision makers instantly if they're preoccupied with "being right" or at least "looking right." Their ego is fear: fear of rejection and being judged by their colleagues. They've built up their self-worth on the perceptions of others. This attitude kills people in the markets as they end up buying high and selling low, based on emotion only. The attitude also kills great decisions in other areas. After all, trading buy and sell points in themselves are nothing other than decisions. People with giant egos are at high risk of poor decision-making, or even if they do it right most of the time, it will catch up with them. A methodical focus on returns gets results.

Good Decision, Bad Results

What should we think of situations in which we followed the best practices of effective decision-making and the outcomes were still undesirable? This is reality. We cannot control everything; we can only control our own approach and actions. Results may vary, especially because other decision makers are taking action—actions that may impede what we're trying to accomplish.

This is a tough scenario we've probably all faced. You take a shot in billiards, which looks like it should work…. and bam… it sucks! This can impact us emotionally. But we have to remember that all we can ever do is make the best decision we can at the time. As long as we're managing our downside, we'll be back at the table to make another decision, taking a different route. This is the normal route to success.

Risk Management

Risk is part of all decisions—a cost that may be the result of that decision. Most people see risk as an external factor beyond their control. That's far from the truth. My experience as a stock and options trader taught me how to completely subdue risk and keep it firmly in our control, which takes away its ability to paralyze us. Actually, even before I worked as a trader at one of Canada's leading brokerages, I read a game-changing book that my Dad gave me—*Trader Vic*. It's dated now, but boy do I recommend reading it. Risk is a central element of the fear that holds us back. Cutting risk down to size is so important to your ability to make decisions effectively.

How do you control risk then? The stock market is seen as super risky, but it's the easiest place to actually lock down your risk. You control your risk 100 percent. Does it sound crazy? If you see it as crazy, it's because you think risk is represented by the volatility of a stock. That influences it, but the risk is actually 100 percent defined by what you set as your exit point. Professional traders systematically exit once they are down 10 percent (their stop loss). If you always cut your losses to this type of level, then you always keep your shirt.

Successful traders are boring risk/reward managers. People will always play up the big swings, big wins, and big fails, but that's sensationalism. It makes for exciting stories, not sustainable profits. So in trading, like most areas of investing, risk is actually directly reflective of the decision maker and the extent to which they let emotion override their risk management. This isn't just theory; I personally learned this over the years. Pause and process this. *You're in control.*

For many, this is an eye-opening perspective on risk. From a CE perspective, it reminds us that we can consistently keep B/C in our favor if we make decisions like an institutional trader rather than a panicked retail trader. In the math of CE, it teaches us that even though we usually face significant uncertain/risk-associated costs, we can also control our C to some degree.

What Is Truly Reality?

Certain and uncertain costs (risk), as well as benefits, do not exist in a vacuum, devoid of human interpretation. There are scientific facts to them, but what every C and B mean to a person depends on their mindset and perceptions. Some people love rain; others hate it. Keep in mind that the C and B you're presented with in your daily life, as well as the C and B you conjure up in your mind, are all subject to your biases—the way you see the world.

So basically, do not take everything, internal or external, literally at first. Think through what underlies the assumptions you're making, and the assumptions others are making. Both represent a lifetime of reinforcement. We all get a little set in our ways. Remember, perception is reality. Beware of it and be aware of your impact on it.

Managing Costs

Our discussion has made a big deal about how benefit follows cost. No pain/no gain and all of that. That being said, the most successful people, especially in business, do not just joyously look for C—certain and uncertain—to bear. They actively try to keep it as low as possible while getting the B they want. Business magnates like billionaires relentlessly try to do business in markets where there's minimal competition, and they seek new business models that take direct competition out of the mix. That's what innovation does. The most successful in these fields find ways to keep C down and drive B up. C is a necessary evil on the way to B. It's not inherently loved by anyone.

Don't Focus Too Much on Others

We've explored how critical it is to take into account the benefits and costs of others in making your decisions effective and sustainable—especially as a leader. We even understood how this is a gap in most other decision-making models. But, I have to caution. Can you imagine that individual who's so clear in their convictions that they think everyone else should share them? We all know people like that. The friend who is a clean freak who judges how clean our place is. Or the one who supports a particular political party and thinks everyone else should too. It's great they have such focus, but they're actually likely to irritate others and undermine causal coupling, which leads to others not supporting them! This reminder isn't trivial. It's easy for all of us to get very excited and consumed by our new clarity in life, making us want to share it with others. We do this unselfishly as we look to help others. It's also great to share amazing things that can help those we care about. The point is to do so without *overdoing* it. Just like everything in life, most principles are double-edge swords. Nuance matters. Balance matters. The ancient Chinese really did get it right with the yin and yang. Beyond a genuine concern for how we come across to others, this is important for us. If we get caught up in micromanaging other people's behaviors for our own satisfaction, we get distracted from actually pursuing our own objectives. This sounds simple, but it's not easy to do.

Getting Better at Decision-Making Is a Decision

You guessed it. Getting better at decision-making must itself be a decision. This book isn't just delivering information that will make you better at decisions. It is introducing you to a proven process that you can execute to get better at decisions.

By this, I mean establishing the STAR elements. What's your sight line for where you want to be based on better decision-making? What specific targets will you hit? What actions will you take and how will you react to ensure you achieve your sight line and targets?

With this in place, is your STAR defined in line with causal coupling—is everyone you need to help you be successful going to also see benefit in line with any costs they may have to bear as a result of your STAR?

Your Decision Web

No decision stands on its own, so don't look at each one in isolation. A whole slew of decisions will build on the same core sight. That's natural and makes sense. I've found it very useful to literally draw a STAR concentric circle diagram for each decision. That way you can see where your sight, targets, action, and reaction items overlap.

How Many Targets Should You Set?

From personal experience and from studying successful people, I've found that targets need to be set daily, weekly, monthly, quarterly, annually, for three years, five years, and ten plus years. I believe you should have a minimum of one major target for each of these time periods. This combination keeps you focused in the short, intermediate, and long term. All targets must be written down and must be SMART (specific, measurable, achievable, realistic, and time-based). You can have more targets than this, as long as you're delivering every day and every week. The number I recommended should be achievable for anyone, no matter how busy they are and how many distractions they face. Everyone has different levels of ambition in their goals. The recommended number matches the individual's targets, no matter what they are.

Do Your Own TEDx Talk

If you haven't come across TEDx talks, you must check them out. TEDx talks showcase game changers in all areas of life: people with powerful ideas and progress in driving change. Whatever you are passionate about, you'll probably find a TEDx talk related to it, which alone is a great reason to learn more. In fact, you can do your own personal TEDx talk, which is a powerful idea for a few reasons. First, this process makes you distill your concepts and action plan into a digestible and inspiring message. Going through this will make you tighten your focus and plan forward. Script your talk out first and have a friend review it. Then record yourself and keep on practicing. For more information, visit www.TED.com.

Where Are You Now?

Your current situation does impact your way forward. The steps required by people starting with very little will be different and much harder than those starting from a much more established position. Making great things happen is actually not easy for anyone, even for those with means. Making great things happen means fighting the status quo, which is always challenging. But if you're facing very difficult times, don't get down on yourself. It's understandable to feel overwhelmed or stalled. It's a challenging journey and you must decide in your gut how much you really want change. If you're in a business start-up situation, you're going to face different challenges than someone in a large corporation. The nature of challenges and hence the nature of the techniques will differ. We'll dive into that more later.

Heuristics

In today's world, often decisions have to be made quickly. Hence, the use of heuristics can be effective when there's no time for deeper consideration or analysis. Heuristics are simple rules we can apply in a vast majority of similar situations because we have found them to work. An example would be "if it sounds too good to be true, it probably is." Have a set of principles you believe in and translate these to heuristics that can be applied. Don't overlook this because they can keep you on track when things are moving quickly. Many experts assert the up to 80 percent of our actual real-life decisions are the result of heuristics.

Know Where Others Are in the Decision Cycle

Always be aware of where others sit in their decision cycle. How well defined is their STAR? Have they hit the level of CODN/BODS necessary for change? This will help you understand and predict what's going to happen and with what level of sustained passion.

How Do You Perceive Time?

You can tell the difference between a person on a mission, going after what they've set their sights on, and a person who's drifting along. It reflects in their intensity, which translates into how they manage, and perceive, time. Their focus gives them an incredible sense of the value of time, so they treat it like a valuable asset more than even money. For people with clear line of sight in their life, money is perceived as a way to obtain the support of others, via their time. For such people, every hour is important and ideally directed at things they value in life. Family, personal development, wealth building, charity, and other areas may earn their attention. To the unmotivated bunch, these people are perceived as not enjoying life or being too busy. On the contrary, they're usually much happier. My advice is to see every hour as valuable and invest it where it matters to you, which can include family time and leisure. Managing time properly with the right mindset lets you achieve your full range of desires, from intense work to relaxed leisure. When you think about, money is just "packaged time." It allows you to free up your time from areas you don't want to apply it, and to transfer those activities to other people who want to do it for money.

Outside–Inside–Outside

Since this is a book on decision-making, it's not surprising that we've spent most of our time looking at our inner mental workings. But we also need to take stock of the big picture process that applies to our perspective on our whole lives. From our earliest days on Earth, we live within the context of a world much bigger than ourselves. It's important to have a highly internal locus of control, but it's naive to pretend you exist in your own world. We're hard-wired to the world through millions of years of conditioning. Your initial inspirations come from what you experience, so stay connected to what's exciting in your surrounding world. Don't become too insular, which is challenging when you're relentlessly pursuing your sight lines. Once you have a healthy relationship with the world around you, you can then focus on your internal viewpoint.

With your internal perspective solidified, you can then give it real meaning by connecting again with the real world. This is when our thinking becomes tangible as we feel visceral connections with the people and action around us. These may sound like small nuances, but I raise them because too many people get lost in their own head or bounce around without clarity. Internal and external perspectives and experiences iteratively interact back and forth. That's nature and our amazing role in it. Savor it. Take yourself and the world around you seriously, but not too seriously.

Don't Do the Easy Quick-Win Tasks First

You might be surprised at my next advice: do not finish off the tasks that fly at you requiring only a few minutes of your time. Not only does this seem harmless, it actually feels good. You're getting things done, right? Why put something on to a to-do list when you can crank it out in five minutes and be done with it?

There are two major reasons. The first is that doing so changes the mindset from doing what's on your priority list to things on other people's priority lists. Each distraction on its own is small, but after a whole day, the snowballing of these distractions is destabilizing. If you're a senior leader, the key is to delegate these instantly, but if they have to be done by you, they should still go on a list, not get immediate triage to highest urgency.

There's a second reason to not let these quicker tasks run your day. Things that seem to be simple rarely end up that way when the layers are peeled back. The process of reacting to other people's seemingly simple interruptions turns your focus upside down and often puts you into detective mode, trying to figure out what information you haven't been presented in order to frame the challenge properly. Hopefully, this has scared you enough to politely triage for priority and urgency and ensure your priorities stay at the top of your list!

Conditioning

The previous discussion on outside–inside–outside reminds us of the connection between our mental and physiological systems. Both systems must be exercised together. Not many people do so with enough rigor. That's what performance experts like Tony Robbins assist with. They put these systems through the paces together, conditioning the mental and physiological to work in unison and on demand. Whether you turn to a true peak performance coach like Robbins, or drive hard on this yourself, you have to practice thinking and doing together and conditioning yourself to spring into action based on that conditioning.

Bounded Rationality

To have a full grasp of Behavioral Economics (BE), you must be aware of the concept of bounded rationality. It asserts that rationality is constrained by the amount of control the decision maker has, his or her cognitive abilities, and the amount of time available. You may have heard the resulting term "satisfiers." Satisficing means that the decision maker seeks a satisfactory solution rather than an unachievable optimal one. Economist Herbert Simon was the pioneer behind this theory, which provides a foundation for much of the subsequent development of BE.

LEADERSHIP

Causal Economics (CE) underpins a powerful leadership style that aligns with impactful and sustainable results. Decision makers who "get" CE always ensure that cost and benefit are coupled. They achieve a sustainable win-win for everyone involved in the longer term.

The idea of decision-making gets thrown around endlessly in discussions about leadership. Leadership isn't vague. It boils down to getting others to support your STAR, while also achieving their own STAR. I'm a big believer in the leadership model put forward by Elena Botelho and her coauthors in a *Harvard Business Review* article.[5] In 2019, they looked extensively at data on leadership from all sizes and types of companies and found four fundamental pillars of leadership. I can't emphasize enough how these insights came from analysis of real data, not speculation from a smart person. The four pillars are:

1. Decisiveness
2. Adaptability

---

5 Botelho, E.L., Powell, R.K., Kincaid, S., and Wang, D. (2017). "What Sets Successful CEOs Apart." *Harvard Business Review*, 95(3), 70–77.

3. Stakeholder Engagement
4. Consistent Results

These are extremely common sense when we read them. Take note that decision-making is the number 1 factor. That's followed by three factors that are also achieved through effective causal coupling.

Let's look deeper at each.

Decisiveness is pretty self-explanatory. Good leaders are good at making decisions. The first part of being good at making decisions is... making decisions. Imagine that. Not to be facetious, but indecisiveness is indeed the biggest barrier to being a good leader. We've pointed out before that no one has all the information they would like when making a decision. Good leaders typically have only 70 percent of information they'd like, according to Amazon founder Jeff Bezos. But they make decisions regardless. Scope is managed. Risk is monitored. Results are measured. Changes are made. A decision can't be improved without action because no new information or insight is obtained without action. In addition, when a leader has this action bias, it sets the pace for everyone else in the organization. If you want to be a great leader, you have to first and foremost become a great decision maker. It's important to keep this simple focus top of mind. Don't complicate it!

Adaptability too is self-explanatory. Most famous corporate failures are examples of inadaptability—Kodak and digital photos, book sellers and eBooks... the list goes on. This factor ties to causal coupling in the sense that the leader needs to constantly stay on top of changing cost and benefit profiles and optimize. There's so much change in the world that it overwhelms most. A great leader will laser in on the implications of change, not all the factoids. This means that all kinds of change from all corners are translated into the common language of incentives: cost and benefit. When a leader thinks in this way, he or she can bring clarity to gravely complex situations. That's critical for decisiveness.

Adaptability ties very closely into the factor of **stakeholder engagement**. Whether or not things are changing, cost and benefit must be mapped out for every relevant stakeholder to a decision, not just a navel-gazing view of the decision maker. Great leaders genuinely invest in relationships and drive win/win/win scenarios that are therefore sustainable.

The last factor isn't too exciting, but it hits home. **Consistent results** are the mark of great leaders. We pay attention to sexy examples of epic home runs and catastrophic failures—because that stimulation is human nature. But that's just sensationalist media. Good leaders are employed by organizations because they drive consistent, reliable results. It does not mean they don't "go big." It just means they can be counted on to deliver. Consistent results mean that investors and other stakeholders feel their benefit exceeds their costs on an ongoing basis. That's causal coupling personified.

A very simple definition of leadership I have used for years is:

- Sights
- Guidance
- Resources

This translates to providing clear sight to the destination, followed by direction on key strategies, and lastly support in lining up necessary resources.

Talk and Walk the Talk

This may be an unpopular one, but today's management mantras have become very fluffy. As CE is built on the importance of causally coupled cost and benefit (change in B/change in C), leadership in a CE context requires walking the talk and asking everyone on your team to do the same. A true leader asking for sacrifices has made proven sacrifices, which explicitly demonstrates that the leader is concerned with maximizing B/C of him/herself and his/ her team. This shows and demands accountability in all directions.

Great leaders are aware of the B/C of their team and they listen and ask questions to gain additional insights. Poor leaders do not take into account the B/C of others and attempt only to maximize their own, through stubbornness. They will undoubtedly talk a good game, but never back it up. This sends a message of lacking credibility that actually undermines leadership.

The action and reaction elements of CE decision theory highlight another common misconception about leadership. People think that leadership involves a lot of followers "on paper." You're not a real leader unless people bear costs for you and take action for you in the face of adversity. Just as important as language is to communication and numbers are to mathematics, the equivalent in leadership is *walking the talk*. Talk is everywhere, costless and empty. Only action earns credibility and respect over time. Which means that one can't be a leader if they just talk.

When is the last time you heard someone in a management role indicate that they don't want to be an inspirational and authentic leader? As many of those "led" will attest to, most leaders talk a great leadership game, but few truly lead people to care and produce amazing results. In the vast majority of cases, this is just a reflection of causal coupling not being met. The team hears the leader say great things and doesn't believe any of it's genuine, based on personal past experiences. They go about their way and nothing changes. Some people are so frustrated with the revolving door of poor leadership that they actively sabotage the efforts of new leaders, so they can be done with their term and return to business as usual.

Leadership only comes with genuinely caring about others, giving first, relentlessly sticking to one's word, and delivering. The principle is simple. But great leadership is tough because of the effort required. In society, management gets easily well compensated for lesser effort, that is, administering instead of leading. However, beyond all leadership talk, there will be a majority of managers with decent results and a minority of leaders with exceptional results. Causal coupling is at the core of this insight, aligning cost and benefit across everyone involved.

Storytelling

When you hear marketing discussions these days, you perhaps hear about storytelling. There are two major phases of communication. The first is "attention" and the next is "engagement"—which rounds out the Interest, Desire, and Action elements from famous advertising acronym AIDA (Attention, Interest, Desire, Action). It's too early to start storytelling when you don't have attention. At the attention stage it's all about an exciting hook that doesn't sound like other hooks. As a leader, you must be good at getting people to turn their ear to you, to want to listen.

Once you have that split second of attention, you have to pounce with storytelling. Storytelling is humanizing everything we talk about here. All the principles we discuss apply. As a leader, you must add emotion and understanding through storytelling. Stories have been the most powerful way to convey passionate messages since the beginning of time. As a leader, you need to get good at them and actually enjoy them. Be human. Not just PowerPoint bullets.

You Are the Pace

You don't "set" the pace through your prognostications as a leader. You "are" the pace by what you do. If you don't visibly move quickly and surely, others certainly won't. As a leader, the biggest things you really do for the organization are demonstrate S and T through clear communications and actions. Your team takes on the A and R relevant to their roles to make it happen. Walking the talk means that you also visibly take on the A and R relevant to your level. Too many leaders don't realize that they actually "report down" to the entire team. They owe regular updates on their own performance to all employees on the same basis as other employees have to report. Good leaders do it more often. This makes everything about *freedom with accountability* (the concept we explored earlier in the book). People have the autonomy to make their mark, but they're absolutely accountable for the outcomes.

You've Got to Couple Benefit and Cost across the Short-Term, Intermediate-Term, and Long-Term.

As a multi-period model, CE thinking ensures that we consider the long term. Sight can be one year out, ten years out, or twenty-five years out. But it should be explicit (written) and specific, especially for others to follow. The strength of a leader's decisions from sight to reaction will inspire others to rally around them. Leaders who ascribe to CE thinking have a refreshing long-term perspective, focusing on current and future impact and even their legacy.

In CE leadership, leaders take their decisions seriously and take time to explicitly map out major elements of cost and benefit into the long term. It's well known that great leaders are able to fail, learn, and pick themselves up to swing the bat again. This reflects CE thinking: the persistent leader ties current failure costs to eventual success. In non-CE models, this cost of failure is the demotivating end of the story.

Always be clear in assigning who is responsible in leading each initiative and give them a chance with measurable timelines and targets, including milestones. If they aren't delivering, change the leader. When you walk the talk as a leader, you're in a position to be direct and fair without hurting morale.

One of the biggest mistakes leaders make is forgetting to align incentives across staff, themselves, and the entire organization. Every individual is rightfully looking out for themselves and their family first. They're used to hearing corporate and leadership BS and then seeing a complete lack of follow-through. Today, people are wary of talk. They watch proposed leaders instead.

Leaders Have to Be Great Followers

One of the biggest misunderstandings of leadership today is that it's different than following. Great leadership and great following must go together. Common perceptions see leadership and following as different things. Even though some positions have more official leadership accountability attached to them, on individual projects team members may be the leader. In a great organization, everyone is a leader in their own sphere of focus.

Partnering

Partnering, especially with other business owners, needs its own discussion. Great partnering doesn't just require leadership or good followership. It occupies a unique position. Jim Treliving, founder of Boston Pizza, lays out some great guidance on effective partnering in his book *Decisions* (I highly recommend reading this one).

Partners have to be peers. Each has to respect the other to play leader, follower, and peer—depending on the issue at hand. Partners must have consistent values and belief systems and very different skill sets. Building an organization? You must take partnering seriously. No one can do everything on their own. Partnering with other individuals who complement you and are just as invested as you is critical to success.

Office Politics Aren't Bad

Office politics are usually despised. That's because we picture the classic example of the arrogant self-centered jerk. No doubt every workplace has such jerks, but it's dangerous to think of this as politics. Politics is natural. It happens when people pursue their own B/C optimization first and then retain some information close to their heart. People who want to keep their jobs naturally have to protect themselves and therefore manage risk/reward to their benefit. It's reality and not really nefarious at all. "Politics," "drama," or whatever you want to call it comes into effect as soon as you put more than one person in proximity. Don't dwell on it. Manage the B/C of others through causal coupling and you'll meet your goals and ensure they're sustainable.

Managing Change

Change management is a well-documented and well-practiced area of business and leadership. One of the most common and dangerous errors in change management is making perfectly logical assumptions from afar about how people need to change. In this view, little focus is placed on why people should truly change and how they can get over the hard parts of change. The "why" comes down to improving the B/C of those impacted and hitting their change threshold. "Why" is a topic on its own, and if you haven't already read *Why* by Simon Sinek, I highly recommend you do. Learning about your own *why*—your sight—and understanding that of others is the foundation of lasting alignment and partnership. Too many leaders make gut-based decisions based on their own self-interested B/C and untested assumptions about the B/C of other impacted parties. CE reminds us to be explicit in mapping out the B/C for ourselves and others.

Emotional State

Change is a great place to look at the role of emotion in our mental state. Consider an extreme example, which may help drive home the point. If you found yourself in a classic horror movie scenario—in an abandoned shack with an axe-wielding psycho—how would your decision-making process be affected? First and foremost, your adrenaline would kick in. On high alert, you'd be making fast, efficient heuristic calculations based on your beliefs about what would work. This would happen because emotional elevation would make sure you made decisions. Your emotions put you into a super-powerful subconscious decision-making mode, with some supplementary conscious calculation.

When your situation is calmer, your emotions and physiology calm down and you can spend more time thinking. This is the mode where comfortable people often fall into analysis paralysis. It's only natural. As we touched on elsewhere in the book, the superconscious is a state where we proactively drive heightened emotions—a natural high, like that of a famous sportsperson—and combine it with elevated conscience awareness, through questions, interruptions, visualizations, and physical triggers.

For many of us, these natural highs are rare in life and all too often come from external drivers, like winning recognition from others, a prize, a lottery, or whatever. When you've landed on your lines of sight and big targets in life, you can get regular natural highs when you make progress. When you're so excited about your end point, you can hit this high every day. I find myself pacing the room each day as I get a natural high about what I'm doing and why. I even have the habit of increasing my pacing speed as I get more fired up. I hope you get to experience the same daily intense highs.

Your current state can ebb and flow. Remember that your current state *will* affect how you make decisions. Your perception can differ on different days. For example, one day you may try mountain biking and hate it. If you try it on another day, you may love it.

Consider how you would make a decision when you're very hungry versus when you've just had a great meal. If you have a big decision to make and don't feel in a positive mental state, hold off on the decision for a while. Or stick to less important decisions if you want to keep the ball rolling. Train yourself to be aware of your current state and what's driving it. You can't fully manage your state if you don't have awareness of where you're starting from and what's influencing you.

Stakeholder States

Much of our focus has been on managing our own mental state for peak performance. But we should also give the same attention to the mental state of the key stakeholders we need to rely on for change. Over time, we strive to influence their states in a win-win fashion as we seek change. However, you have to be completely aware of their current state. It's not an exaggeration to say that sometimes people just aren't in the mood to listen to anything. When individuals are very angry, frustrated, hungry, and so on, they usually are overwhelmed by that emotion and associated thoughts, and are not receptive to anything else. In this case, there's nothing you can do besides support them. That could earn you some trust slowly. Only once their negative state has deescalated can you have an impact through directed change and leadership. If you do the opposite and try to directly reason with someone not ready for change, you'll make it worse. They may see you as a threat and put up barriers in resistance.

To change people who are on a very different page than you want them to be, you have to manage them through the NAC process. You earn their trust by first being aligned with their beliefs and values. Then you gradually expose them to opportunities to discover new belief associations, which are only slightly out of line than their current beliefs, and which show B/C improvement, especially with very, very, very low C. This starts momentum in a new direction, momentum that can build steam and become reinforcing as they begin to process new information with their modified confirmation and selective perception biases.

But all of this initial momentum is just a primer. It won't accelerate or even stick, until you eventually crank up efforts to demonstrate massive C (cost) associated with the status quo. In addition, there must be a new perception of massive B (benefit) associated with the new target outcome. Let me be even more specific. You can't just crank up B/C perceptions in new situations and C in the current situation. C has to hit and stay at that person's personal total cost threshold (change ratio). The change ratio is semipermanent, or sticky, for various reasons. It can change, but in the short to medium term, it's like a wall. Think of something you're scared of—heights, public speaking, speed, being an outcast…. anything. That is your wall. Imagine if you felt that wall every minute of every day. That's when you are guaranteed change.

Consider the classic success story we've probably heard: of the very poor kid who faces crime and depressive circumstances every day. His/her family is at risk in a tough neighborhood that has no jobs but more crime. Many could fall victim to this, but there are those few who hit a pain threshold. They do not tolerate this status quo and work very hard to become a great athlete, an entrepreneur, a religious leader, etc. They escape their restrictive environments and excel because the pain of the status quo was so high. Some of the most inspirational stories are those that unfold in this way and then the successful person gives back to help others up.

If you don't know your walls, you don't know yourself well enough. If you think you're invincible and have no fears, you're certainly sheltered. We are ALL humbled when vulnerable. Driving change is very hard work. True leadership is very hard work. It takes a time investment and an underlying belief that you can help someone to a better place.

People Don't Change Overnight

It's probably pretty clear at this point that inspiring others to change is hard work and takes time. Even if you've done everything right through NAC, behaviors take time to change. It's really important to keep this in mind, so that you don't get frustrated by the pace of change and throw in the towel.

Don't Be So Collaborative

Be wary of today's trendy management ideas. Many have become too soft for maximum results. When it comes to execution, there must be importance placed on a more directive approach. There's too much ego-stroking happening to make everyone feel important every minute of every day. Professional management spends a huge amount of time on "perks" and "kudos" that don't tie to results. Management meetings are often sessions where leaders enjoy hearing themselves speak, not really hearing the others; everyone walks away with expectations of others, without significant expectations from themselves. This reflects leaders who maximize their own short-term B/C without appreciation of the B/C of others and longer-term appreciation for the organization. This isn't really surprising. Professional management is usually compensated for short-term impact, which is a great example of causal decoupling in management thinking. Shareholders should demand more causal coupling from the organizations they invest in. The ideal scenario is when professional management is well compensated for really strong results. Compensation and perks can be very high; they just need to better tie to results in many situations.

Get Ready to Make Some Enemies

Driving change will ALWAYS earn you enemies. Your enemies will be those benefiting from the status quo. That's because the status quo didn't just arise from nowhere. It's the result of people pushing their own vested interests forward. Such people expect quid quo pro from the status quo in return. It's natural that change will face resistance. Some inexperienced leaders seem surprised by this. Let me be very clear. There will always be resistance to your desired change. If there isn't, you're not really changing anything of substance.

As a change agent, the only thing you need to do is be aware of who the roadblocks are, have your case prepared against their objections, and enlist more influential support than resistance. This is not a one-time endeavor. It's a constant, and occasionally painful, fight. Ensure it is managed as best as possible. Don't forget that many people gain benefits beyond cost in their current situation. They are strongly motivated to undermine you. Likewise, there are others who can benefit from your change. Enlist them and fire them up as vocal supporters.

Your Colleagues Have to Lie to You and That's Okay

No one will tell you the full truth. Get over it. It's not a slight on you. No matter how great you think your culture is, people have families to feed and they're dependent on their incomes. They have to walk the party line and for the most part nod to whatever corporate stuff comes down the pipe. Don't waste time with corporate talk. Be fair. Take action and follow through on your own commitments and you'll earn maximum trust and performance. Measure people on their actions, reactions, and results. Don't get caught up in too much talk.

What If You're Already a Solid Leader?

Many of you readers are already great leaders and powerful decision makers—especially if you're a senior executive with a lot of accountability. In many ways, this forces us to make decisions. So if you're great at making decisions and do it all the time, do you need to understand CE, BE, or any such thing? I believe true masters always want to be on top of new developments that affect their skills so they stay as sharp as possible and ahead of competitors. It's hard to think of a better place to have an edge over others than that of powerful decision-making.

Talk Tornados

We've all met people who constantly use vague talk to keep actions and reactions at bay. As a leader, this is the far larger risk than clear and identifiable saboteurs. "Talk tornados" occur when individuals who don't want to change ensure that an initiative is hampered by great conversation with no concrete targets, actions, or reactions. This behavior makes it look like something is in the works, but ensures that nothing actually gets done, leaving the status quo intact.

Decide or Die

We've all heard of analysis paralysis: delaying a decision out of fear of being wrong. Analysis paralysis can occur due to fear of the loss implied by being wrong or the loss of ego of being judged by others. Either way, it's highly destructive. This isn't some kind of rah-rah observation. It's cold, hard reality. If you aren't feeling great about your decision, the only way to improve your perspective is to move forward in obtaining more information. You can't learn by doing nothing. You need to act, which allows you to learn, practice, and obtain additional information, which can help tighten your options.

People usually never have complete information, and they certainly don't if they are stationary. Ironically, those who think they have all the information they need are usually those with huge egos, which are too big to admit they can learn and make better decisions over time. The big ego maniacs are very often the worst decision makers.

Are You Really a Leader?

Leadership is so often characterized as hiring people smarter than yourself, inspiring them, and getting out of their way. This is coaching, not leadership. In such environments, the talent usually ends up "cowboying" it and doing things that don't always align with company objectives. This occurs due to a lack of depth in the supposed leader's understanding of the situation. Even worse, such cheerleading doesn't do what a leader should do—provide a vision, strategy, and resources, and help clear some organizational roadblocks.

Leadership versus Management

The terms leadership and management get thrown around interchangeably far too often. We all know the difference in our gut. It's nothing to do with rank, title, or role. Managers administer in a bureaucratic manner. Processes are how they think. Leaders think about people, and so they inspire, guide, and support. Teams tolerate managers due to their power, and do the minimum expected from them. On the other hand, teams follow leaders with passion and excitement, putting in more than is expected of them. Let's be very clear. Leaders can drive exceptional change. Managers never can.

Respect

Great decision-making doesn't just benefit the decision maker. It indicates respect for others. There's no stronger demonstration of respect for the time of others than making great decisions. Making poor decisions consumes others' time and complicates things for them. It's disrespectful to not use time wisely when it impacts others. Be proud of your decision-making and the positive impact it will have on others around you. Respect goes two ways. As a decisive person committed to your goals and having respect for others, it's absolutely fair for you to expect respect from others. There are people who will feel refreshed as a result of your confidence and there are those who will resent you. The latter have an opportunity to share in your mission. If they're barriers, move on.

Respect the Decisions of Others

As we intensely focus on our future, the best of us may naturally become a little self-indulged. That's why it's important to actively demonstrate respect for any decision—your's and that of others. When it's another's decision, especially when someone on your team makes the effort and steps forward to expose themselves to scrutiny, it's critically important that you explicitly acknowledge the courage and the decision. There are two reasons. The first is to build trust with your colleague to encourage more of the same behavior. The second is to publicly "revere" the act of decision-making. At every turn, you want decisions to be the activity that is placed on a pedestal. That's what helps change culture over time in support of your leadership.

Your Decision Style

So much of business is rightfully based on relationships and even friendships. This builds trust, which can reduce risk and improve working collaboration and comfort. I'm a big believer in this approach. BUT, too often this spills over into the area of decisions, resulting in a casual approach that produces a lack of specifics. Sight, targets, actions, and reactions may become sloppy. Discussions between good friends and associates are laidback, which means that it's hard for decision makers to get serious. It can be a buzzkill to get serious in such a situation. I truly believe that the best leaders and decision makers are able to achieve this balancing act. They are liked and respected and move back and forth from laidback to serious.

Leaders in various disciplines can take remarkable insights from good sales leaders in this regard. Sales teams always walk this balance. Good salespeople genuinely pursue relationships that benefit their clients, themselves, and their employer. They of course put their own needs first (as they should since they're human) and seek to build value with others. In addition, there's a transparent, direct, and serious aspect to targets and decision-making.

In an effective sales team, there is complete clarity on the team sight and targets. It's called quota. I believe that the sales culture is something that should propagate more into other areas of business. The only risk in this regard is that short-term thinking can occur, as sales numbers are short term. But the sales culture is a great starting point for getting alignment right. The way to tie that to longer-term results is to infuse additional longer-term bonuses and/or equity for defined results.

Trust and Transparency

One of the most fundamental implications of CE is on communication. Specifically, CE reinforces the fact that credibility and trust are built through transparent interactions over time. Lifetime customer value and depth of relationships are entrenched in this manner. If this sounds like nothing new, that's because these concepts get thrown around a lot, but very few organizations truly deliver. Take, for example, marketing communications. Marketers will talk a great game about being transparent in their value proposition and being focused on long-term customer value. But they'll immediately turn around and develop communications that demonstrate ONLY the upside to their solutions. How often have you seen a marketing campaign that covers the reality of implementation, admits to negative customer experiences, or even talks frankly about pricing? So much for transparency. True transparency is rare. And people wonder why trust is too.

Another manner in which CE lends communication a fresh perspective is leaders going deeper than headlines. With shrinking attention spans and message overload across most audiences, it's hard for marketers, politicians, and others to go deeper than repeating headline-level messages that keep people focused and minimize risk of countering the message. The problem is that most messages being provided today are empty. Buyers and voters are left without any specific details to evaluate. They have to turn to actual experience to judge beyond the promises.

Creativity

People often mysticize creativity. For our purposes, let's keep things crystal clear. Creativity comes from combining ideas in ways not yet done, which produces new ideas. Ideas don't fly out of the sky. Creative ideas are actually a systematic generation of alternatives without judgment. They should be very different from status quo and yet close to status quo. Both "big leap" creativity and "incremental" creativity are necessary, powerful tools. If you don't think you're creative, you can practice. Anyone can develop their creative abilities.

Think Fast and Slow

Nobel prize-winning psychologist and economist Daniel Kahneman developed the powerful idea that short-term crises situations require a different level of thinking than the long term. One should not apply the same type of thinking to each. In the longer term, slow thinking allows us to build out C and B more fully and boost the rationality of many of our decisions. In the short term, slow thinking will result in not making decisions and potentially disastrous consequences. This being said, be careful of thinking that's too slow. Speed in decision-making is key as we've touched on, so analyze quickly, make a calculated move, measure results, and adapt.

Planner Doer Models

A reputed two-stage model is put forward by Richard Thaler. Two-stage models are powerful and popular in psychology and neuroscience. In a model developed by Richard and Hersh Shefrin,[6] decision makers have different modes of short-term and long-term decision processes. In the short term, they often myopically maximize only current utility. In the longer term, they are also forward-looking planners looking to maximize lifetime utility.

---

6 Shefrin, H. M., and Thaler, R. H. (1980). *Rules and Discretion in a Two-Self Model of Intertemporal Choice*. (Graduate School of Business and Public Administration, Cornell University, New York).

Personal Rules

Decision-making is a systematic process. Hence, we recommend using some simple formal frameworks to direct your thinking. This includes STAR and other checklist types of tools covered later. Don't take them for granted.

Put Your Toes in

One of the important things to remember in decision-making is to dip your toes in. Tackle big decisions with smaller decisions first and build up to the big one. This way, you can measure results and alter course to keep your shirt and nail down opportunity. Big, risky, scary decisions garner all the attention. These are merely fiction, created by sensationalists who don't understand what really goes into a decision. Success stories are not made overnight as the headlines like to portray.

Be Careful with Business School

I'm not downplaying business school. I had the honor of attending elite schools for my MBA and economics degrees and they taught me a lot. That being said, the focus is often on analysis, not decision-making—even in schools that use the case method of discussing and analyzing real chronicled business situations. Though brilliant, some professors can't truly teach you real decision-making because they are career academics. You can only practice business decisions in reality, so pay attention to professors that have done what you want to do. If you really want to get better at decision-making, it's best to start a venture on the side and practice with calculated exposure.

Personas and Profiles Aren't Just for Marketers and the FBI

Marketers take great care to understand their target markets. They write out buyer personas, identifying demographic and psychographic factors in their thinking. This process helps them uncover insights into why and how they may buy, and potential barriers to purchase. The FBI and similar organizations profile targets they are after, with the same goal of predicting behavior through a deep understanding of individual drivers. As a decision maker, if you want to make great decisions, you should add these tools to your arsenal. They aren't just for cops and marketers. Only once you truly understand your buyer's B and C drivers can you communicate effectively to their needs. And only then can you seek to influence their behavior and nudge them toward purchase.

Stop Trying to Be Right All the Time

One of the biggest signs of losers is they're people who are always right—in their mind. This is not humanly possible; it simply indicates that the decision maker is not open-minded to learning new things that could help optimize decisions. I learned this as a stock trader. It was actually quite predictable as to who would make money and who would lose money in the long term. The long-term losers spent their time talking up their super smart trade that no one else had figured out. They were driven by their ego of being smarter than everyone else with the big-win trades. The long-term winners spent their time cutting losses when their stop losses were hit and reinvesting for another trade.

Success is sexy once it's achieved and everyone wants in then. Success is boring in the build phase and nobody cares. Should you always pretend you're right, or can you manage C and B trade-offs to improve your position slowly and surely, without ever having your entire war chest at risk? A great way to practice getting this right is to compliment others more often and not just play up what you do.

Always Have a Plan B and C

No one's plans are perfect. This is a simple reminder to take the time to explicitly devise a plan B. Better yet, devise a plan C too, to stay ahead of your competition, who may anticipate your plan B. When big stakes are on the table, this is what your competitors will no doubt do. Keep these plans to simple STAR bullets so you can act quickly.

Create Your Own Choice Set

Marketers take great effort to persuade decision makers by framing the choice set available and the relative attractiveness of each. It's a great idea to apply this thinking to yourself. Create your own choice set like a marketer does. This formality helps you focus. And yes, it's okay to influence yourself. That's what we do when we manage our B and C for our best results. Defining a choice set just makes it easier to decide by pointing to a very specific alternative. It removes vagueness around what to do next. You're kind of marketing the best decision option to yourself, so you do what's best for yourself.

Decision^x

When you've made a great decision, you're on track to remarkable outcomes. Imagine if you combined that with other decisions. Some decisions will align with others in a way that's essentially additive. By working with others, you can help each other and end up with more than your individual share. But imagine if you were able to align with multiple other decisions makers, whose decisions directly aligned as part of yours? In that case, you can get an exponential impact. Think of your decision to the power of x. That's really how people scale. When you think about organizations and teams, where the power of the group is higher than an individual's contribution, this is essentially what's going on. This is extremely important to remember when decision-making as a leader.

THE DECISIVE ORGANIZATION

Decision Competency

An organization's success is directly tied to its ability to make decisions. The history of innovation illustrates that most declining organizations fail as a result of not making bold decisions that keep up with or drive change, and not as a result of brave decisions in the wrong direction. The latter case is exemplified by many companies, including famous tech companies, which pivot when their decisions are shown to miss objectives.

There's no momentum without decisions. But it's easy to talk about decisions. How do we ensure to not fall into the same old trap, where we get excited about our new insight and then go right back to our old habits? We have to be able to measure decision competency at both individual and organization levels.

It's for this reason, working with companies, that I created the **Decision Competency Index (DCI)** to get to the heart of this challenge. People can be certified to conduct DCIs (CDE: Certified Decision Expert), as can organizations (CDO: Certified Decisive Organization). You won't be surprised that this cannot be measured through surveys. There's no room for intent and wishful thinking. The DCI can only be calculated based on unannounced third-party observation. Companies that want their DCI calculated place a certified DCI analyst into some of their projects, especially meetings. This analyst will join the team in a "cover role" so their real mission remains concealed until completion of the DCI initiative.

Decision competency can be measured on a few parameters, whether the decision aligns with clear:

- Sight (overall destination)
- Targets (outcomes, costs, speed, risk thresholds)
- Actions (is there a plan, is the plan sufficient, is it being met?)
- Reactions (do they keep us on track to the areas above?)

It's easy to measure decision competency because either there is a well-defined decision against which to measure performance or there is no decision, which is a failure in itself. To formally measure DCI, we rate and average at least 100 decisions, where each of the four factors is measured on a scale of 0–10, and the four scores are added. Individual DCI scores therefore range from 0 to 40. For organizations, an average is calculated like this across all employees, showing the scores for management and frontline employees.

We've worked with the rare company where some people react to this as an intrusion. They are quite frankly wrong and this reaction points to culture issues regarding lack of accountability. Employees are hired to work for an organization and make the necessary decisions, including actions that achieve goals. No employee should feel that measurement of these skills is a problem. Everyone should conduct themselves openly and in line with company interests at all times. Any problem with this approach is an excuse. A person's private life needs to be respected as private. Their time at work is literally on the employer's dime and there's nothing wrong with an employer measuring effectiveness. Employees have no right to expect that they can do things at work that others shouldn't be privy to. If this process were public, behaviors would change as people try to come across as better decision makers.

If an organization wants to measurably improve its DCI, it can employ a certified DCE facilitator who will get involved in projects, meetings, and email chains to facilitate improvements in decision competencies of individuals and the organization. After such exercises, organizations typically conduct a revised DCI measurement. In this phase, meetings are transcribed/recorded and the analyst reviews from outside, to ensure that their now public presence doesn't impact behaviors again.

Some organizations opt not to explicitly measure DCI, but instead just implement DC training. This is a very pragmatic way for them to realize the power of decision-making competency and realize from casual observation that it can be improved at their organization and in key individuals. Having key staff achieve their Decision Expert Certification recognizes and rewards this critical behavior and sets a visible public standard for others to follow.

What Do Organizations Typically Get Wrong?

My thoughts here might fly in the face of much of modern business hype. But I've found the biggest problem is usually a largely undiagnosed condition of "too many cooks in the kitchen." Think of your organization. There's probably clear accountability around who owns what department, specific job roles, and so forth. But beyond operational stuff that neatly fits into departmental buckets, change initiatives are usually driven by market needs—either demand or competition. Are there committees in your organization where everyone is super important and takes up a lot of airtime? Give everyone some initiatives to lead across departments and some to support other leaders as a contributor.

Group Decisions

Oops. There's no such thing as a group decision. Only individuals have brains and can make decisions. People can align around similar decisions and groups are statistically dangerous to decision-making. It's not that groups are inherently bad; they're vital to the leverage and scale needed to drive results. The problem is that many businesses' poor decision practices make groups dangerous if not properly managed. The reason decisions in a group context are higher risk than fully individual ones, is that people naturally think and act differently in groups. They often nod support for those with more power that they rely on—especially their boss. This is often a real concern for job stability. People justifiably often say things they don't believe, because they have to feed their families and because power structures may be misaligned. For every decision, there needs to be "one throat to choke" or "one back to pat"!

Teamwork

I might offend some readers here. But my comments are driven by a focus on getting your desired results—they aren't about sounding great. It's much easier to be great at CE leadership when you're operating on your own. The reaction phase can be tough as you engage with others, but you're driving the other prior steps so they hit less external resistance. It is in many ways harder to be effective at decisions when you have to work with a team across all stages, from sight to reaction.

You will find examples where you're right and believe in your sight but have to put up with others taking the floor with worse approaches. For all the talk of diverse views today, the reality is that there are fewer great ideas and tangible plans than there are unwarranted opinions and time-wasting banter. The 80/20 rule applies: 80 percent of people won't be at the level of contribution you need. That's a combination of brains, experience, and attitude.

I'm not here to spread happy vibes, which you can get in any other business book.

Causal coupling is clear. People need to step up and contribute, and reap rewards based on that. Too much management thinking is based on pandering—talking the talk of political correctness and the greatness of having so many voices. If your goal is to win political correctness points, that's your business. Let the best shine, no matter what their background is. Be open to all views, but evaluate them quickly and be clear and fair in communicating your feedback. If your goal is to drive the line of sight you're passionate about and see it to fruition, you need to keep the agenda focused on it with some supplementary but managed input from other sources.

It's a catch 22 though, as you need to be on good terms with everyone at the table when it comes to rolling out the final decisions. And even though open discussions involve a lot of waste, getting feedback is critical, as even the most brilliant, well-thought out plans have scope for improvement. It's best to keep your team membership tight to those whose feedback will be truly relevant.

Remember, in teamwork, talk is cheap. Give people the credibility they deserve as a result of their actions over time. It's fashionable not to judge others. I believe it's absolutely fair to judge people by their actions relative to their commitments. And if they make no commitments, that's just as bad.

Intermediaries

One of the key takeaways of CE and the principle of causal coupling is that the further removed cost and benefit become, the higher the risk of ineffective decisions. In our complex economy, there are many intermediaries that get in the middle of interactions. Intermediaries can play an important role, but be aware of the risk they pose. I don't mean this particularly nefariously, just that as intermediaries like government, corporations, associations, unions, NGOs, or industry Self-Regulatory Organizations get involved, causal coupling can break down.

When causal coupling breaks down, the core incentive structure breaks down, putting fair and sustainable outcomes at risk. With big bureaucratic intermediaries in the middle having their own objectives, those that contribute sometimes don't see rewards and those that benefit from the intermediary policies don't always have to contribute accordingly. Keep this in mind within your own network and organizations. Is causal coupling strong and keeping incentives in line, or are bloated intermediary bureaucracies and processes punishing contributors and rewarding freeloaders?

Process

We're used to operating in an environment where we get caught up in a minutia of details. We check our calendar, task list, voicemails, and more. This reinforces an external locus of control and distraction. I believe that decisions—defined by STAR—should be the first thing we define, and from there we can access and work with the data from different perspectives. Typical lenses include time (calendaring), tasks (attached to a project), owners (activity owner), dependencies, and priority decision listing. Placing formally defined decisions at the center of your thinking and planning puts you in control and sets you up for success on your terms.

Software

I am excited to be working on a decision-making support app that brings the insights of CE and STAR into practice to help you make better decisions. This software has a number of improvements over other options out there. Typical productivity software contains calendaring, tasks, contacts, and email. These are disjoint interfaces. The CE•STAR software is centered on the decision itself, defining

S, T, A, and R. Calendaring, task lists, and so on are, as a result, just different views into the decision. This structure makes it easy to follow decisions through to results and to allocate them across teams.

The true power of this approach is possible today thanks to AI (artificial intelligence). AI assigns tags to all information to append it to individual decisions. These tags allow the central decision entries to be spun into different report views. Once you start entering some core representative decisions, the software will use AI to predict and assign appropriate tags that people normally don't take the time to add.

If you're interested in evaluating a beta version of the CE•STAR decision-making app, reach out to our publisher at contact@ascerian.com.

Inertia

Before we dive into the functional department areas of business, let's make a surprising defense of inertia. We all know inertia is bad, right? Well, it certainly feels like the opposite of decisive action. But there's a twist worth mentioning—from an organizational perspective. The power of organizations is that once they reach critical mass, they keep on going. This contributes to the frustrating bureaucracy we all feel with them, but we generally overlook the powerful upside of this inertia. Once an organization, with its people, processes, and technologies, is in action, it will keep on ticking. You don't have to relaunch all those things each day. This continuation of momentum outweighs the bureaucratic barriers we all hate, but since we feel pain more than pleasure, the latter is what sticks with us.

Organizations deliver scale, which is absolutely required to achieve big results. In the end, their benefits usually exceed their costs. So build and let the train keep on rolling. Then tweak it as you need, through a focus on decision-making competency.

Sales

Most salespeople believe they provide value before asking for the business, but it's often not true. Too many of them interrupt potential buyers and ask to assess needs, which actually reduces value. The salesperson asks for time upfront and does not offer any value upfront. The pressure they face of short-term quota targets makes this a common behavior. A large number of sales professionals believe they're building great long-term relationships when they're in fact demonstrating a self-interested transaction, interruption approach. The latter reduces value and makes potential buyers look elsewhere, which explains why those potential buyers who seem hot go with an alternative option in the last minute. The bottom line is that you have to first *give*. Don't start by asking for time to assess and sell. There's no value to your customer in going through an assessment with you. Don't forget this.

Many fields have some form of an 80/20 Pareto rule, separating the exceptional from the run-of-the-mill. That's a cold reality in most areas of nature. In sales, this distinction is more acute than other areas of business. In sales, there are those who make incredible amounts of money and the rest who don't. The difference comes down to attitude and behaviors—essentially the decisions that the exceptional ones make versus the ones everyone else makes. We know this because sales isn't an area that requires certifications and structural hierarchies that determine pay. It's the purest form of causal coupling, attaching pay to results.

Is Your Team Selling Selfishly without Your Knowledge?

CE also sheds light on the way one sells. Ineffective sales executives usually reach out cold to prospects and ask for time to ask personal questions to assess whether there's a sales opportunity.

There is no *give* first. It is a self-centered, rude interruption. Add to that, options and pricing are kept mysterious to protect the seller. It's shocking that people actually sell this way. It results in 100 percent of time and risk costs falling on the potential buyer and 100 percent of potential benefits in the process accruing to the potential seller. No wonder that this type of cold, zero-value selling performs so poorly.

So what does it mean for you or anyone you know who sells? Reach out to potential buyers with a complementary offer of value. This isn't a be-all-and-end-all, as a lot of BS offers sound like this as well. Wherever possible, work referrals before cold contacts. This lowers risk. Just offer value and back off. Give them time. Aggressive follow-up adds no value to them and undermines your credibility.

I find it ridiculous when someone prospecting me actually asks if I'd like them to follow up in a week. Why would I want them to do that? Of course I want to reach out when I'm ready. And I know they're going to anyway. So it just makes everything seem so obviously artificial. Drop this silly question of whether you should follow up. This isn't the same as trying to get the next meeting into the calendar right away. If you're adding value, getting a follow-on meeting into the calendar keeps up momentum for both of you.

These examples illustrate how the nuanced thinking of CE and causal coupling can improve our understanding of our potential customers and our behaviors in seeking to build profitable business with them. Just like BE and nudging are in many ways nuanced formalizations of what marketers have always known—as pointed out by marketing legend Phil Kotler—CE is a nuanced perspective that gets better results. But as we know, nuance is at the center of all great results. Lots of us go to the gym. Few of us look as buff as "The Rock" a.k.a Dwayne Johnson.

Marketing

Market Research

CE warns against research surveys. Surveys capture intent, which is usually not closely related to actual behavior. Instead, techniques like "camping out," taken from Stage-Gate methodology are suggested, to best match cost and benefit in action. This will offer true insights into your buyer's view, which includes a broader perspective of C and B on personas outside your traditional sphere of consideration.

Segmentation

What a simple concept, right? And we all do it. So what's the big deal? We touched upon market research, and that fuels proper segmentation. After doing proper market research, you'll have a clear picture of what motivates your potential buyer. Make sure you actually draw out their B and C into two columns. The additional point to make about segmentation is to make it behavioral. So much of segmentation for so long was all about demographics, not psychographics. Demographics can be convenient shorthand that captures a number of implicit behavioral drivers, but don't consider them as more. This point is so important that I usually break the convention that marketers have of naming their segments on key demographic traits and instead name them by key behavioral traits that underpin everything.

Buyer Personas

CE reminds marketers to get out of their own heads and into the full perspective of the potential buyer. This sounds simple, but it's truly rare in practice. It means that the marketer considers all the cost and benefit factors impacting the buyer, even those that don't directly involve their product or service. Only in this way can costs and benefits be fully accounted for and tied together, allowing the marketer to offset each cost with benefit.

Attitude

CE is centered on the principle of coupling cost and benefit for everyone involved. *For everyone involved.* This core win/win is what makes things sustainable, as no one is incentivized to counteract the outcome. In marketing, this has deep implications. It may sound "cheesy," but truly successful companies have to really and genuinely care about their customers and prospective customers. This means being interested in them for who they are, not just as part of the process toward a purchase. The amazing brands we all love became who they are because they had this perspective and it came through in how they designed and delivered solutions.

Lifetime Customer Value

Another area where CE often opens the eyes of sales and marketing professionals is that of taking a long-term perspective. This means going beyond the single transaction with a forward-thinking perspective, which includes transparent communication. Conventional wisdom suggests that salespeople and marketers just sell the benefits. That's BS. Every potential buyer knows that your solution includes benefits and costs (beyond price), both literally and relatively. If you position your solution as just benefits, without any downside, including implementation challenges and if you don't clarify how it really relates to competitors, you're not being honest with potential buyers. That means you're transitioning costs and research effort to them without being upfront. The bottom line in this case is a lack of trust and lower referrals, references, and long-term purchases.

The ultimate business example of causal coupling is a long-term partnership based on mutual value between a brand and a customer. Mutual value is a paramount distinction here because some long-term relationships paraded around are based more on market dominance by a brand.

To fully match cost and benefit, an entire lifetime horizon must be considered. This leads to the importance of nurturing with great content. Sales and marketing professionals routinely talk of the importance of long-term relationships. But many do good work and just expect loyalty, instead of systematically overcoming personal total costs with aligned personal total benefits.

Persuasive Communication

This is the big one, right? Everyone wants to be better at reading minds, anticipating moves, and getting ahead of customer needs and competitor actions. This can be mastered. But most people don't take the time to understand and apply the basic psychology involved in decision-making. Even more interesting is that the vast majority of people telegraph their thinking all the time, so their decisions can actually be quite easy to anticipate and preempt.

CE has big implications for communications. We can think of decision-making as a language in a way. If you believe that making decisions is just as important as talking, why would you believe we need a common way of speaking and not a common way of making powerful decisions that we all understand. Such a common framework makes it easier and more efficient to make decisions and carry them out, as individuals and organizations.

As mentioned previously, to build relationships, deep trust is required, which only comes with fully transparent communication. Most sales pitches and marketing today are not fully transparent. Rather, they position just upside benefits with no costs. CE suggests that companies should be honest about the costs of implementation and how they can be overcome as an example. It boldly means that companies must also be clearer on where competitors are known for some strong advantages. But this has to be done carefully so as to not frame a bias against your company. Communications must be truly transparent to build trust and accelerate conversion—from value proposition to campaign copy. Honesty about implementation is one of the best things you can do to build deep trust and credibility.

Nudging

The most famous insight from the increasingly popular area of BE is nudging. Nudging is an explicit influence on people's voluntary decisions by making preferred choices more beneficial and less costly/risky to a potential buyer. In many ways, this is also the definition of marketing. Behavioral economics backs it up with strong science. CE produces a similar concept: coupled nudging, which is nudging that also meets the criteria of being causally coupled—with costs and benefits for the prospective buyer being matched over the entire decision time horizon.

Pricing

Don't be mysterious with pricing. Once you have a basic sense of qualification, you should give guidance pricing. This reflects a CE view where all parties are seeing returns and value for their invested time and efforts. Many experts believe that communicating pricing too early sets expectations that could be way off base as more information comes to light. This is true if very specific pricing is given before needs have been assessed. It's fine to avoid doing that, but waiting too long to provide range pricing and pricing parameters is an example of causal decoupling that will erode trust in your potential customers.

Some companies that otherwise have an understanding of the great value they provide become arrogant and start to feel that price doesn't matter because their value is so great. That's crazy. Value to a customer is the ratio of benefits to costs—including price. Every dollar spent in one place is a dollar that can't be spent in another vital area. Never take price and your buyer's budget for granted, no matter how great your people are and your solution is.

If you do, eventually a more understanding competitor (often an upstart) will wipe away your smugness.

The Customer Isn't Always Right
What? Isn't this one of the most fundamental rules of business? The idea is a good one, but context is critical here. Customers are just people. They would love to have your solution at no cost and have all the extras thrown in. They are very busy and budget constrained and bombarded with BS, and hence displace their pressure on you. They're usually unrealistic, most often in budgeting—that is, if they're spending their own money and not someone else's of course. The mantra that the customer is always right is good for keeping us focused on meeting their needs. Make sure you take this away from it, but know that they're usually not right and in many complex B2B situations they need to be diplomatically educated on everything from issues to options.

Framing
In the end, marketers are concerned with framing their solutions in the best possible light, which aligns with potential buyer needs and conveys how their solution is a better choice than alternatives. Framing is the perceived context faced by decision makers. Marketers try to present information that frames the decision preferentially toward their offering. The most powerful way to frame is to present B/C scenarios aligned to desired outcomes. When marketers try to influence buying decisions, they use priming in an effort to achieve favorable framing. Priming is the process of planting conscious and subconscious information to steer a decision maker's focus. This priming aligns with the concept of nudging contained in BE as developed by Richard Thaler.

When a specific item like an image or number is used to frame perspective, it's called an anchor. Another powerful technique is putting a negative halo around alternatives that you want avoided. Good marketers present at most five to seven alternatives so as not to overwhelm. They may also provide decoy/dominated alternatives that won't be chosen but make the decision maker feel that the other ones are better options. For example, super high and super low prices may be presented, knowing they won't be chosen, but they'll leave the decision maker feeling strong about the middle price, which could be higher than optimal had it not been framed this way.

The endowment effect is also a powerful method of framing. Give people something for free and they won't want to lose it. No one wants to give anything up. That's why free trials work. Experience via a trial also lowers the risk of the unknown. The power of free also applies here. Once you have a potential customer engaged through a free trial, it's much easier to move them to purchase.

Price is a signal of value. If you price your product too low, you'll convey to the market that your value delivered is too low. Price it too high and you'll come across as elite and only be attractive to the niche market that values that.

Credibility

Credibility, along with its outcome, trust, are possibly the most important areas where CE and causal coupling deliver a very distinct insight from traditional theories. Most of the world experienced by potential buyers is one of BS. Almost every piece of sales and marketing communication today is a flow of information about the benefits, but not the costs of solutions. No one believes it and it slows down the buying process as the potential buyer now has to do their own unbiased due diligence. Credibility can be *earned* through *authority*—based on one's title/position, for example. It can also be earned through social proof, such as testimonials and case studies. Regardless, it always comes with an honest and transparent coupling of B and C in commercial communications.

Referrals
Most businesses do their early building through referrals. This means that new business can be brought on without the cost and effort of finding a new customer. Referral programs are an amazing strategy. Here it suffices to point out that referrals only come with the highest levels of trust. People only vouch for who they trust. Organizations that do a great job at referrals take great care to be more transparent and responsive to their customers, ensuring they reduce C and increase B relative to alternatives.

Transparency
Closely related to credibility is transparency. Transparency is important in marketing communications to build credibility and trust. Very few organizations have the courage though to really do this well. True transparency that earns intense trust involves an honest presentation of the challenges involved with a solution, especially when it comes to implementation. If you look at most marketing, you see the opposite. For example, technology is complicated, but technology marketing makes implementation and support sound almost effortless in many cases. Potential customers don't believe it and its omission casts a shadow of doubt over other elements of the value proposition. When an organization takes this very seriously, they'll even be upfront about the total costs faced. For example, some costs can be triggered even beyond the company's own solution. True transparency means these aren't ignored. It means they are addressed with meaningful, not always easy, approaches.

Account-based Marketing
Account-based marketing (ABM) has gained well-deserved traction in recent years, for high-value complex solutions. These solutions have long sales cycles and buying committees with differing incentives. For these top-priority, big ticket accounts, it doesn't

make sense to mass market. CE applies more to ABM than many other areas of marketing. It's the ultimate exercise in matching B to C at each stage to move the process along. Whenever C gets in the way, or is expected to get in the way, the marketer can infuse some helpful B by various means, to lower fear and other C barriers slowing down the buying/sales cycle.

Free Trials
Earlier we discussed the endowment effect from economics. We noted that even if people were given something for free, once they considered it to be their own, they didn't want to give it up, even though they didn't pay for it. Marketers use this as one of the most powerful marketing methods out there—giving a free trail. This lets people experience the solution and reduce fears about it and it also kicks the endowment effect into gear, so people don't want to give it up. Free trials can be effective for solutions that are easy to experience—like products. It's difficult to provide free trials with highly complex, custom-built solutions. This is because the experience is hard to recreate without massive investment and because the results can differ depending on implementation success and other factors. In such situations, case studies often serve as the closest thing to a free trial.

Funnel Building and Customer Journey
Marketing, like sales, is all about persuasively conveying value and differentiation over alternatives. That means that many of the points raised in the discussion on sales apply to marketers. What are some of the differences specific to marketing? One nuance is that marketing generally has to do a lot more communication earlier in the buying process. Sales executives for the most part get involved when prospective buyers are ready to talk to a person. Prior to that, buyers are researching on their own with minimal intrusion. This is where marketers have to earn relevance and credibility.

Marketers who follow the principles of CE take great effort to map cost and benefit at each and every stage of the buyer journey. This exercise makes clear where breakdowns in conversion flow are occurring and highlights where marketers/salespeople can intervene to lower C obstacles and increase B motivators at such choke points.

Content Marketing and Inbound Marketing
Content marketing is all the rage today. But so much of it is done poorly. By poorly I mean that it's often a thinly veiled sales pitch—self-centered, tied to product features, not needs exploration and strategy formation. As recommended in previous areas, content marketing that aligns to CE is client-centered, very transparent on pros and cons of alternative approaches, and conservative in projecting benefits.

Sales and Marketing Alignment
A realistic discussion on marketing, at least in a business-to-business context, isn't complete without the never-ending issue of sales and marketing alignment. Sales and marketing can always talk a great game on alignment, and politically speaking they have to. But it's usually a cover. As Stephen J. Dubner and Steven Levitt taught us in *Freakonomics*, people do what incentives drive them to do. These incentives align with cost and benefit. Salespeople are compensated on the deal. That's where they make their real money.

As a marketing leader, you can drive deeper alignment with your sales team and sales leadership by evaluating causal coupling at every phase of the relationship. How can you claim to be aligned when your team doesn't have any significant compensation tied to winning deals?

Internal Communications
Meetings, emails, phone calls: these are the most common communication methods used in business today. They're also loose and

contribute to sloppy decision-making, perhaps more than anything else. Language itself is a great standardization tool to allow efficient interaction, so why do we stop at language and allow these other tools to be so undisciplined? Compare business emails to another alternative—academic papers. The latter are structured and follow such rigid protocols that they're only accessible—to both create and read—to technical people in the specific field. Thousands of small incremental enhancements are made to slowly move along a body of knowledge, tightly controlled by insider peer reviewers.

This system produces solid progress over time, and acts as a barrier to true breakthroughs. This barrier can be overcome, however, by the best ideas. If business emails were like academic papers, not much would get done and innovation would certainly be squashed. There's a good balance between these extreme examples of loose and tight communications. Have meetings and emails that follow an agenda shared in advance with action items that are regularly and visibly followed-up on, relative to the STAR framework. It isn't rocket science; it just takes effort.

Corporate Social Responsibility

My goal isn't to get political here, but since companies and individuals are put in the crosshairs today by activists—for causes, noble and farcical—leaders and organizations have to be vigilant. Can CE share insight to help?

Today, communications are weaponized as highly emotional messages propagated over social media. The emotional approach can paint the target as "a bad guy" regardless of facts and differences of opinions. We've seen big brands get brought to their knees by this negative publicity from professionals in the "outrage industry."

What causal coupling does is highlights that the activists are exploiting the target's fear of large brand costs to motivate supporting actions that cost less. For the target, the benefit of compliance is avoidance of huge damages to the brand, which far outweighs the explicit cost of supporting the activist's requests. This is brand extortion.

Activism is a pressure tool and can be good or bad depending on the mission. That's why analysis matters. However, activists are always certain that their agenda is the only acceptable approach, typically based on a combination of ideology and personal gain. A company or individual rarely comes out ahead in such battles.

The Future of Sales and Marketing

I believe the future of sales and marketing is aligned with a deeper understanding of CE. That's because we continue to see these areas evolve in line with buyer needs. Marketing used to be all about interruption. Then we saw the birth of content marketing and inbound and permission-based marketing, concepts that moved marketing toward buyer preferences. Buyers have pushed back a lot of the untargeted interruption they face. They expect marketing to be tailored, helping them get value easier and earlier. This reflects better alignment of cost and benefit for buyers. Costs are reduced through less interruptions, and benefits are increased through a better fit of communications. Companies also benefit from better causal alignment, because they're putting costs directly to where the opportunities are, lowering overall costs, and getting the benefit of selling more to accurately targeted audience members. ABM is the future of marketing.

Service Delivery

Customer Satisfaction

$X \geq 1$ is a powerful, tangible way to determine whether your clients are satisfied. Are they seeing B/C with you that exceeds what they would experience with alternatives? If they're not, you're in trouble, and it's a matter of time until they defect.

You should constantly talk to customers to see and document where their B and C sit. This gives you a structured way to evaluate what their comments actually mean in terms of potential decision-making.

Human Resources

HR decision makers can apply CE to improve their decision-making.

Employer Brand Differentiation

The brand that an employer presents to potential employees is just as important as the brand presented to potential customers. Some companies feel they have to keep these brand perspectives identical. But they must be nuanced differently for every different audience or they won't be relevant. That doesn't mean that core principles aren't the same. It just means that different audiences—prospect customers and potential employees—need to hear different things emphasized. Causal coupling reminds us that to properly nuance these perspectives, we must segment them based on their B and C profiles.

Compensation

One of the strongest examples of causal coupling that already exists in business is performance–based pay. The company bears a cost directly aligned with the benefit of the delivered performance. The employee earns pay directly aligned with the delivered performance. This is very clear in sales teams, where a large part of pay is tied directly to sales quota performance. Where can causal coupling shed additional light? More roles can be compensated based on results. Critics of this assertion often argue that for non-sales roles it is hard to compensate on outcomes not as explicit as sales, which are not controlled by individuals. This is a large theoretical error that's existed in business for a long time. CE shows us why it needs to be eradicated even though it sounds noble.

In a perfect world, it would make sense to compensate people only on what they can control. In the real world, no one controls anything fully. Sales people don't control customers and can't be sure what exact outcomes will result. Every role at every level, can beyond some safety net base, have extra pay tied to results that they influence. That they don't directly control everything reflects the very nature of why people are needed in a role. They need to stickhandle others to drive results. If something doesn't need a person to drive it to an outcome, then it can be automated. This doesn't imply everyone's existing pay should convert from fixed to variable. It means that people, from frontline staff to executives, can make more based on driving performance. Targets can be achievable milestones of progress toward an outcome that is itself too big to quantify.

Unions are an emotional topic when it comes to compensation and related issues, but CE sheds clear light on how they can work for everyone. There are certainly examples of where they protect employees from horrible employers (however, labor legislation does a lot of hard work here), and there are certainly examples of how they destroy potential productivity through bureaucratic rules. The number one way unions could be properly aligned to be fair to employees and employers is to switch from a seniority model to a performance model.

Seniority is a weak proxy for performance and is often inversely related due to incentives. Unions should protect workers if they protect the vast majority who are great contributors and want to provide for their families. Workers who don't add value or drag on results should not be shielded by unions, regardless of seniority. This switch would make the union model fully in line with causal coupling. In a similar fashion, nonunion roles must be compensated for performance in their reviews, rather than for their "qualifications on paper" like their degrees.

Commission Can Be Done the Wrong Way

No-brainer alert. Commission pay is always a win/win for sales executives and their employers. Although this is not always true, and many organizations have learned it the hard way. Revenue isn't always profitable, and that's why pricing never sits with sales. You can imagine a sales person giving away solutions with no profit to make larger revenue numbers and get paid more commission. This would end up maximizing benefit and minimizing cost for themselves.

Training

HR can play a key role in advancing decision competency. One of the biggest ways is by providing all customer-facing/customer-supporting departments with decision competency assessments and training. Even though HR can play a key facilitation role, buy-in must be broad across the executive team and functional department leaders.

Equity

Equity is the ultimate form of compensation for effort invested. It's the best way to align potential returns to those who invest the required costs in terms of time and money. Equity is tied to long time horizons and the risk that goes with it. With fair vesting terms, it does the best job possible of aligning results with effort in the real world—where many others are often "in the way" to some degree of a perfect world.

We Need More Followers in Organizations

Where CE flies in the face of a lot of modern management rhetoric is the suggestion that we need more followers in organizations. This isn't negative. All of us should lead the initiatives we own. That means a CEO and an executive assistant should each be leaders on particular initiatives and own them end-to-end. Each is just as important as a leader on their initiative. It means that the CEO should publicly be a following team member on the initiatives owned by the executive assistant. There's too much talk of everyone being empowered and important on everything. This ends up with too many cooks in the kitchen pontificating and doing things their preferred way.

Roles and Teams

One of the biggest fails in organizational structure is a lack of clear roles on teams. There needs to be one meeting facilitator who can set the rules with the complete support of senior leadership. Importance of a particular person in a particular meeting on a particular project should not necessarily tie to importance in job titles. When this is breached, people are too polite and worried about repercussions to call out how bad it is. When roles on a team aren't defined by business purpose and accountable project leader, people just love to hear themselves talk. The loudest and most powerful make a lot of noise and everyone just goes and does their own thing.

A Lost Communication Opportunity—Email

Before we slag on email too much, don't forget that before email there was what we now call snail mail. We used to just call that "mail." Email was a breakthrough communication that brought tremendous speed. Overall email is great, but the challenge is that it's used less formally than old-school mail. This means loose language, which is a challenge when we can't rely on face-to-face to fill in the gaps in context. People can also ignore email, which they can also do with other communications. Relevance remains first and foremost. Beyond that, email can be powerful if it is structured into a format that efficiently brings analysis, options, decisions, and follow-up actions to the forefront. The elements of a good email are:

- Goal of the email (what and by when and any other metrics)
- The reasoning behind the ask
- Next steps (what you and others need to do by when)

A Huge Barrier to Decisions—Meetings

Most meetings lack structure, let alone structure conducive to decision-making. They usually involve everyone jockeying for airtime, so they can hear their voice and earn nods from others. The pushiest get heard, not the best ideas. Power structure also drives who gets airtime and whose ideas get the most default support. In meetings, social etiquette also gets in the way of what can be said. Every comment is the result of careful political positioning and signals to support allies. In most cases, everyone comes to meetings with a view and leaves with the same view.

It's not that meetings have to be this way. We're picking on meetings, but they're really just a symptom. The real problem is poor discipline in managing meetings for what they're supposed to do—reviewing options, making a decision, acting, and reviewing. Meetings are expensive time investments and should be carefully facilitated. The meeting should be seen as a very expensive proposition and managed professionally. This can be done by internal leaders with proper training, or by calling an external professional facilitator. An organization doesn't have to turn to hiring expert facilitators on an ongoing basis. They can have CE facilitation experts train internal experts (like PMO employees), as long as senior management empowers them appropriately.

So how can meetings be effective? The biggest improvement is usually in the process format. Many senior business leaders will scoff at templating things like this. They are wrong. Just as we rely on common words in language to communicate, we should be able to rely on a recognized discipline process in something as important as a meeting. Leaders who react negatively to this have blinders on because they're used to having the floor based on power surrounded by nodding heads who go through the motions without conviction.

So what does effective meeting facilitation look like? Overall, there needs to be a defined facilitator for each meeting. You have your most expensive talent in the room for many meetings, so why wouldn't you treat it like professional consultants do when they come in to your organization. The facilitator must aggressively interrupt the meeting regularly and bring it back on track. Each meeting should have an agenda and post-meeting documentation, which includes sight, targets, actions, and reactions—both pre and post. This is the master format for great meetings. It's not extra work; it saves work. If your team finds interrupting tough, they can practice the interruption format to get comfortable with it.

Purpose

Invitations to meetings without an agenda are inexcusable. Even if you're a CEO. This is a slap in the face to invited attendees. It proves that the organizer doesn't value participant time. They won't say anything, but they come with this perspective in their heart and mind, which already has them thinking about the work they have to get done, not the proposed meeting. Many of us are so used to this type of disrespect that we have to pause and remind ourselves how bad this is. If you're trying to formulate a sight, then it's okay to not have a sight included in your agenda. But if you do have a sight in place and this meeting supports that sight, it should be included. If targets exist, they should also be clearly reiterated in the agenda. This constantly places focus where it needs to be. This may seem like a trivial nuance, but it's critical. You get what you measure as the saying goes. Your targets are measurable, so you better have them explicitly aligned to a similarly tangible sight. This is one of the biggest factors driving ineffective meetings. The takeaway—HAVE A CLEAR AGENDA WITH YOUR CURRENT SIGHT INCLUDED.

If these sound in any way like trivial semantics, ask yourself how productive is the average meeting you attend. Innovative meeting formats can make a big difference. Just ask the Queen—I believe her Privy Council conducts meetings standing up—which fosters brevity. Small change. Big impact. What can be done at your organization?

Let's take a look at some of the specific elements of meetings—what works and what doesn't.

Pre-Prep

We've all witnessed the most disastrous of meetings where no one has had time to prepare. Everyone is busy, but it's not acceptable to schedule meetings that people don't have time to prep for and it's also not acceptable to show up to meetings without preparation.

Facilitation

Before, during, and after. Everyone is busy and politically vested to manage follow-up. You need a facilitator to keep meetings on track and convey follow-up steps.

Post-Meeting

As most of us know, the meeting itself addresses 1 percent of what needs to be done. It's easy to talk and sound smart. Post-meeting is where the other 99 percent comes to bear. I emphasize this not so you don't take meetings seriously. They are key. My point is that most people get all caught up in the meeting like it's way more than 1 percent of the effort. Meetings where people have the wrong weighting in mind don't give enough attention to the key milestones required during actual implementation, after the conversations are over. As someone who understands the longer-term relevance, where B and C are matched over time to drive successful rollout, you can ensure that realistic plans are mapped out.

Innovation

Innovation is one of the strongest business applications of CE and causal coupling. It's a priority for executives trying to reinvent existing markets or uncover new ones. Innovation represents the ultimate upfront investment through time and capital. It's the example of clarity of sight and goal setting—in a world where goals may need to pivot regularly. And these examples are just once the business is off the ground. Coupling goes to the heart of the innovative idea process itself, where individuals invest massive amounts of personal cost in anticipation of a huge future benefit.

Just as decisions often get confused with thinking, innovation often gets confused with ideas. Coming up with ideas is fun and almost everyone conjures ideas in the shower or over a cup of coffee. Ideas are important, but in terms of commercializing and operationalizing a concept, the idea just scratches the surface at the "sight" stage. Targets, actions, and reactions represent the hard work that needs to follow.

CE provides major insights into the source of ideas. Too many new business ideas come about from very smart people ascertaining a need based on solid logic. This is one of the costliest approaches one can take in reality. Ideas should only ever be conceived as a result of observing actual buyers in the field paying to solve a problem and not getting what they want. Only then can the innovator observe where the target market is truly willing to bear the cost of paying for proposed benefits. You can't guess what people will actually pay for. They themselves can't even predict what they'll actually pay for.

That's where CE gives us additional insights into buyer behavior and the dangers of relying on market research surveys that only measure intent. Intent is a long way away from actual decisions because it doesn't involve action and reaction. BE faces this challenge as it invokes lab-observed insights that don't reflect the real world. With a CE mindset, we instead realize that we need to immerse in the environment of our potential buyers.

Personal Decision Assessment

We've invested a lot of our focus on assessing organizational decision competency, but how do you do the same for your own competency? Isn't that just as important? It sure is. We recommend that at least annually you conduct your own PDA (personal decision assessment), selecting your favorite and worst decisions and assessing each against the STAR elements.

EMERGING AREAS

Personalization

Businesses continue to focus on moving from mass marketing to complete one-to-one interactions. Personalization is the ultimate goal of marketing, where C and B components of the value proposition can be altered in real time to facilitate purchase, among other things. This might be the biggest way in which causal coupling and CE can impact the future of marketing.

For example, in location-based marketing, instead of just suggesting things nearby, imagine automatically showing the fastest way there, the best route, and any relevant special offers. This is slashing costs/barriers in real time. Imagine in a complex IT deal that white papers and testimonials are presented in real time to address obstacles that the buyer is signaling in the buying process. These are examples of personalization innovations in action. Companies that do this are pioneers in CE and perhaps don't even realize it.

Artificial Intelligence (AI)

It's hard to find a bigger buzz word today than AI or artificial intelligence. AI isn't a fad, but as with most cool innovations, the buzz is a bit ahead of the current potential. If you're not up on AI, it's actually really simple. Data are analyzed for relationships and then software learns from these relationships, building iteratively and improving over time. This central element of machine learning is what characterizes AI. The better the data and greater the opportunities to explore and learn, the better the predictions that can be acquired. In this way, AI can to some degree simulate human intelligence.

AI can teach us about our own decision-making in some important ways. It emphasizes the approach of being "open minded" and reviewing lots of data for new and interesting trends. AI can help at this stage because the computer can be programed to avoid a number of the biases a person would exhibit at this stage. A real opportunity to incorporate CE into AI is to align AI analysis more to human decision structure where all data are mapped to C or B, reflecting real human biases.

The real opportunity with AI is for it to provide baseline decision support, upon which human thinking can be optimized. This parallels the way many other technologies are thought of—they supplement what we do. From a CE point of view, AI can take time-consuming and calculation-intensive tasks from a person and move them to a machine, leaving high value and high benefit thinking to the individual. This provides a positive B/C gap, which gets fairly closed by the cost of obtaining the AI.

CE TOOLS

Now that we've covered the core principles and major applications of CE, it's a great time to summarize the tools you can use to apply it. I'll also explain each of them in detail.

Keep It Simple
Forget massive step-by-step plans. Keep your main plan to one page only. Otherwise you'll find it hard to squeeze in ten minutes here and there for continual review.

Personal
The tools provided here are meant to bring sight, targets, actions, and reactions to the top of your mind, to interrupt the interruptions if you will. Tools are just tools however, and I've got to be upfront in reminding you that if you truly believe you're onto something new and powerful, you have to take up the cause in your own mind. Tools can only help. Nothing in life can replace *you*. That being said, here are some that have been tried and tested in action and shown to provide stellar results.

The CE One Pager

I've personally used this tool for years and it's helped me balance family, career, side businesses, investments, and the many other projects I'm passionate about. My headspace literally goes from one world to an entirely different one throughout the day. Changing gear so quickly means a complete mental and behavioral shift for a short window of time. It takes a lot out of people to cross back and forth between various intense mindsets. Not surprisingly, I'm going to suggest a tool that keeps our STAR top of mind at all times. It's the CE One Pager.

I keep an electronic copy of my STAR in Google Keep, so every time I check my phone I see it. We all know how addictive we can be with our phones. Turn that into a positive. While many people do constant phone checking for external feeds, successful people do it to check in on their STAR. Most of us say we're too busy, but then somehow magically find time every thirty seconds to check our phone. What this really means is that we're too busy reacting to external distractions to prioritize our own STAR. This comes down to the fact that most people have a dominant external locus of control, letting society define and direct them. Successful people, as defined by themselves personally, always have a dominant internal locus of control. Your One Pager must include daily, weekly, monthly, quarterly, annual, three-year, five-year, and ten plus year targets.

Decision Log

People who get things done are very clear on the most strategic decisions they've made and the status of each. If you're a board chairman, you might have a only a handful of very high-level decisions to make and manage. Your decision log has to allow you to track results regularly. That's common practice for many. What we add to the decision log is the ongoing tracking element. I feel it's very important to track how quickly you're making decisions and moving through the STAR phases.

NAC (Neuro Associative Conditioning) Plan
We discussed NAC earlier and here we include it as an official tool.
We suggest a written NAC plan beside each decision in your log.
Just lay out in writing the NAC stages for each major STAR decision.

The Change Ratio (CODN/BODS or Personal Total Cost Threshold)
For each decision, in addition to documenting your STAR, it's vital
that you document your current change ratio. This metric may
increase or fall and where it sits helps you to be explicitly aware of
how fast you're going to get to your sight for success.

Three Squared Rule (3:9:81)
You may see the ratio 3:9:81 used by active practitioners of CE.
Wondering what it means? It's pretty simple. This is the typical
ratio of sight to targets to priority actions that some gurus use in
their planning. It's not really a tool on its own, just a guiding piece
of wisdom in forming your decisions.

Personal Decision Assessment
Identify your best and worst decision within the last year and analyze each based on the SMART criteria. Don't dwell. Just do this to
uncover blind spots you weren't aware of, as well as areas where you
already excel in the process.

Superconscious Triggers

- Print a photo of someone or something that inspires you
  the most in an area you enjoy. Put it in your wallet as a visible photo. Put it on your desk and add it to your One Pager.
  Look at it at least ten times every day.
- Come up with three power questions that require innovative answers from you in your area of interest. Ask them and
  answer each of them at least three times a day.

- Ask the questions and look at the photo together and at the same time envision yourself in the scenario you've framed up.
- Put a reminder of where you don't want to be as well.

Organizational Perspective

An organization's success can be improved through decision-making effectiveness. An organization is a collection of individuals, so I recommend that the individual tools noted be implemented for success. Organizations also become more than the sum of the parts—culture comes into play. A macro view of the organization is key, as is conveying a macro understanding of decision-making. Beyond individual tools, here are some pragmatic tools an organization can use.

Two-Step Discussions

One of the biggest barriers to progress in interactions is the way dialogue goes in today's culture. Typical discussions parallel political discussions. People are trying to "be right," arguing their agenda and driving discussion down endless rat holes that support their points and disarm competing points. Most discussions are not discussions, but rather competing agendas trying to hog the airtime to monopolize and generate supporters.

The two-step discussion process minimizes this through a simple structure.

1. One person has five minutes to make their points.
2. The other person has five minutes to rebuff the first person's points (not other points).

This goes back and forth as things get fleshed out.

Decision Competency Assessment

This involves an expert assessing the individuals, processes, and structure of an organization, to identify the impact on causal coupling and decision-making. An organization can either develop an internal expert or engage a DCE (Decision Competency Expert) certified consultant. See CausalEconomics.com for certified practitioners.

Decision Competency Training
This involves an expert delivering corporate training, either to a select group of key leaders, or more broadly—to improve decision competency following the principles introduced here. This training differs from most forms of corporate training in that it requires an ongoing commitment to check in on progress, due to the importance of follow through on A and R in the STAR framework.

A SNAPSHOT OF CAUSAL ECONOMICS DECISION-MAKING

If You Remember Only Four Things from This Book… What Should They Be?

We've covered a lot of ground and deep dived into a number of areas. How do you remember it all? My recommendation is to remember four primary takeaways from this book.

1. **CAUSAL COUPLING (Incentives):** Understand that incentives (costs and benefits) drive all behavior and that decisions can't be modelled with traditional neoclassical economics and Behavioral Economics—outcomes are not random, whether rational or not— they require upfront cost (deliberate and risk) followed by anticipated benefit, which is the principle of causal coupling at the core of Causal Economics. It is captured via $X \geq 1$ for the individual.

2. **STAR (Management Framework):** Make your decisions explicitly within the STAR framework.

3. **CHANGE RATIO (Change Management):** Always know your change ratio (CODN/BODS) and that of others. No change happens until this threshold is hit.
4. **X $\geq$ 1 (Sustainability):** Ensure all your decisions provide X $\geq$ 1 for all key stakeholders.

A Summary of Major Principles to Remember

- Rationality (we are all rational and predictably irrational)
- Causal coupling for individuals (B follows C)
- Causal coupling in society (X $\geq$ 1 for all involved)
- STAR (Sight, Targets, Actions, Reactions)
- Know your CODN (cost of doing nothing) and BODS (benefit of doing something) and CODN/BODS at all times
- Success requires an internal locus of control
- Seek trusted external advice
- Generate three plus alternatives
- Interrupt yourself regularly
- Decisions include actions—act
- Keep your life One Pager and decision log with you at all times

A DECISION EXERCISE ROUTINE

We mentioned earlier that decision-making is first and foremost an acquired skill—acquired through practice. Anyone can have the decisiveness of a powerful CEO. The scale of the decisions a CEO has to make add intrigue, but it's really the same. Building your decision-making expertise will take repetitive practice—practice of the right types of skills. We recommend that you complete the following one-month decision fitness program:

- *Week 1:* Create your One Pager to include your core sight across family, health, personal development, financial, career, legacy, and so on. For each decision, develop the STAR elements, three potential decision choices, the CODN/BODS ratio, and take immediate action.
- *Week 2:* Create a decision log that contains each item on your One Pager (columns are decision, sight, target, actions, reactions). For another three decisions, develop the STAR elements, three potential decision choices, the CODN/ BODS ratio, and take immediate action.

- *Week 3:* For the rest of the decisions in the log, develop the STAR elements, five potential decision choices, and the CODN/BODS ratio. Take immediate action on all five of them. You are now up to one well-directed, well-actioned decision a day!
- *Week 4+:* Continue with this process every single week, but increase to three decisions each day. Keep this as your ongoing minimum.

A Helpful Challenge

I know that even if you fully buy in to the principles of this book, it takes time to change your perspective and behaviors. I've mentioned earlier that analyzing and learning from your previous decisions is a vital way to move forward. With that said, it's hard (well, impossible) to objectively assess your own performance this way. So that you're not left hanging, we've set up a very popular way to help you. If you've read this book end-to-end, then you qualify for our supporting offer of personal assistance. If you send our publisher (publisher@ascerian.com) an example of what you consider to be your best decision and an example of what you consider to be your worst decision, our team will review and provide personalized one-on-one feedback, so you can truly learn from your own experiences—objectively. We need not just a description of your decisions, but also an assessment of what you think you could have done better.

KEY TAKEAWAYS

Given the formal grounding of our topic in the economic theory of CE, this book may not have been "a fun by the pool" story. If it was for you, please let us know!

It's time to ask whether I've helped you get clarity on your life and what you want to do with it. Better yet, what are you currently doing with life and what are you going to do next with it. If I've left you with a belief that decision-making (including action and reaction) is the most important skill you can have in life—because it's the only thing that translates your unique passion into being—then I'm thrilled!

I'll end with a challenge. Do your One Pager now. Take a look at it at least three times a day and make at least three decisions each day from it. Life is awesome. Have a roadmap to keep it awesome. And remember that the road we all take is really just a string of decisions that build on each other.

So what's your final thought?

BE DECISIVE!